MAKING IT WORK

SOCIAL PROBLEMS AND SOCIAL ISSUES

An Aldine de Gruyter Series of Texts and Monographs

SERIES EDITOR

Joel Best
University of Southern Illinois, Carbondale

Joel Best (*editor*), **Images of Issues: Typifying Contemporary Social Problems**

James A. Holstein, **Court-Ordered Insanity: Interpretive Practice and Involuntary Commitment**

James A. Holstein and Gale Miller (*editors*), **Reconsidering Social Constructionism: Debates in Social Problems Theory**

Gale Miller and James A. Holstein (*editors*), **Constructionist Controversies: Issues in Social Problems Theory**

Philip Jenkins, **Intimate Enemies: Moral Panics in Contemporary Great Britain**

Valerie Jenness, **Making It Work: The Prostitutes' Rights Movement in Perspective**

Stuart A. Kirk and Herb Kutchins, **The Selling of *DSM*: The Rhetoric of Science in Psychiatry**

Bruce Luske, **Mirrors of Madness: Patrolling the Psychic Border**

Dorothy Pawluch, **The New Pediatrics: A Profession in Transition**

William B. Sanders, **Juvenile Gang Violence and Grounded Culture**

Malcolm Spector and John I. Kitsuse, **Constructing Social Problems**

MAKING IT WORK

The Prostitutes' Rights Movement in Perspective

VALERIE JENNESS

ALDINE DE GRUYTER
New York

About the Author

Valerie Jenness is Assistant Professor of Sociology
at Washington State University.

ALDINE DE GRUYTER
A division of Walter de Gruyter, Inc.
200 Saw Mill River Road
Hawthorne, New York 10532

This publication is printed on acid-free paper ♾

Library of Congress Cataloging-in-Publication Data
Jenness, Valerie, 1963–
Making it work : the Prostitutes' Rights Movement in perspective / Valerie Jenness.
p. cm. — (Social problems and social issues)
Includes bibliographical references and index.
ISBN 0-202-30463-9 (cloth : alk. paper). — ISBN 0-202-30464-7 (pbk. : alk. paper)
1. Prostitutes—Legal status, laws, etc.—United States.
2. Prostitution—United States—Moral and ethical aspects.
3. Coyote (Organization)—Political activity. 4. Sex and law—United States. I. Title. II. Series.
HQ125.U6J46 1993
306.74'0973—dc20 92-43845
CIP

Manufactured in the United States of America

10 9 8 7 6 5 4 3 2 1

This effort is dedicated to women who rebel against being controlled through the imputation of deviant labels, as well as the consequences that such labels induce. Although they stand at the margins, may they continue to push at the boundaries and serve as an example and inspiration to others. And, of course, may they be successful.

Contents

Acknowledgments

Three sources of funding contributed greatly to the production of this book. The Schlesinger Library at Radcliffe College provided financial support for this project when it was in its "formative stages." Likewise, the University of California financially supported this work through two travel grants, a Social Sciences/Humanities Research Grant, and an Interdisciplinary Humanities Grant.

Facing the task of formally acknowledging all of the individuals who contributed to this project is almost as intimidating as facing the task of writing a book. It is difficult to keep a comprehensive account of the debts I've incurred in the process of maneuvering through the various phases of the production of this book. Thus, I will no doubt fail to mention people who contributed to the completion of this project. I can only hope that I've already informed them of my appreciation in a less formal manner.

Many people have assisted with the so-called technical aspects of producing this book. The staff of the Schlesinger Library was generous with its time and skill while helping me gain access to COYOTE's organizational documents. Alex Chisolm in particular was helpful with data collection during my stay at the library. She photocopied thousands of delicate documents and ensured that I obtained the information I needed to construct an empirical record of COYOTE and its crusade. Just as the staff at the Schlesinger Library was invaluable, so too was Donna Poire at Washington State University. She deserves not only my thanks for repetitively double-checking, formatting, and printing the manuscript, but an award for her patience as well. I appreciate her mild teasing on the seemingly endless occasions on which I said, "Trust me, we *really* are almost done." Finally, Richard Koffler and Arlene Perazzini at Aldine de Gruyter provided useful assistance in the final stages of putting this book together.

As a sociologist, I have been extremely fortunate to be surrounded by supportive and talented colleagues. The most direct contributions to this project came from Naomi Abrahams, Bill Bielby, Joel Best, Joe DeMartini, Sarah Fenstermaker, Ryken Grattet, Armand Mauss, Tamotsu Shibutani, Malcolm Spector, and Beth Schneider. I am deeply indebted to Beth in particular for her extraordinary unselfish support over the years. From the beginning to the end of this project, she has generously devoted far more time and attention to my work than anyone could reasonably expect. In addition to her invaluable substantive advice, she reminded me to meditate (which I *still* haven't done) and maintain a sense of humor (which I *still* can't do without).

As I wrote this book I have benefited from the intellectual, social, and personal support of many family members, friends, and colleagues, especially Laura Appleton, Leslie Atkins, Ed Bassin, Mike Bonner, Debbie Curran, Shoshanah Feher, Melanie Gay, Deborah Haynes, Marilyn Ihinger-Tallman, Shirley Jackson, Cheryl Lepper, Averell Manes, Lisa McIntyre, Harvey Molotch, Julia Mullen, Wendy Simonds, Jan Stets, Noel Sturgeon, and Charles Tittle. Individually, these people have enhanced my personal and intellectual life in unique and dependable ways. Collectively, they managed to create personally and intellectually rich environments for me to revel in—something truly greater than the sum of their parts.

I owe a special thanks to the leaders of COYOTE, Margo St. James and Priscilla Alexander. Margo made this work possible by listening to her heart, offering her voice, and "calling off your old tired ethics." Priscilla made this work possible by trusting me enough to rummage through her office, ask endless questions, and write COYOTE's story from a sociological point of view. Both have been extremely patient with me as I progressed from naive to whimsical to analytical, and not always with the substantive concern(s) they would have preferred. In short, I am extremely grateful for their ongoing willingness to refrain from telling me to get lost, which no doubt crossed their minds on numerous occasions.

Finally, I also owe a special thanks to Lassie M. Bonner, my friend from birth. Although she hasn't always understood what I was doing, she's always trusted my judgment, respected my abilities, and supported my efforts. Support such as this only comes from a mother who, without hesitation, thinks her daughter is simply wonderful—despite an abundance of evidence to the contrary. Perhaps the best thing about publishing my first book is that it provides me with the opportunity for self-indulgence, in this case a forum to say "I love you, Mom" publicly.

Foreword

In 1965, Edwin Schur published *Crimes Without Victims,* arguably one of the most influential critiques of social policy ever written by a sociologist. Schur attacked laws against abortion, homosexuality, and illicit drugs, arguing that criminal laws against such deviant exchanges were unnecessary and unenforceable. Schur's arguments were repeated when movements for legalized abortion, gay liberation, and decriminalized marijuana took off during the early 1970s.

As Valerie Jenness notes, claims about the futility of laws against victimless crimes also became part of the rhetoric of COYOTE—the most visible organization in the contemporary campaign for prostitutes' rights. Of course, COYOTE had other sources of inspiration, especially the new women's movement. COYOTE attacked vice laws as old, tired ethics which victimized women by making a crime out of what should be treated as work.

While COYOTE received some favorable publicity, its claims have had little effect on public policy. In part, COYOTE had trouble forging an effective alliance. Many members of the women's movement defined pornography as a central force in women's oppression, and they were reluctant to take up the cause of sex workers' rights. The AIDS crisis created another fear—that prostitution might become an important vector in spreading the new plague. Few policymakers saw advantages in making a public alliance with COYOTE. In the face of these concerns, the prostitutes' rights movement found itself stalled.

In practice, policies against abortion, drug deals, sexual sales, and the other deviant exchanges Chur called crimes without victims tend to treat customers and sellers differently. The customer is viewed as foolish, or perhaps desperate. In contrast, the seller is seen as more experienced, more knowing, and more culpable—someone who exploits the customer by taking money in return for tainted, harmful goods. This imagery is hard to shake. For nearly two centuries, prostitution reformers have tried to shift the blame, arguing that prostitutes are often young and poor, women with few options, whose male customers knowingly abuse them. Reformers often advocate publicizing the customers' names, thereby making the men's deviance visible. But these campaigns have had little effect; the police and courts continue to pursue supply-side policies—punishing the sellers, while largely ignoring the customers who demand the illicit services.

COYOTE's rhetoric sought to construct prostitution in very different terms. COYOTE rejected the language of blame, insisting that prostitution should be viewed as a normal business. COYOTE further presented itself as the prostitutes' voice. Unlike earlier prostitution reform movements, COYOTE did not just speak on behalf of prostitutes; rather, it allowed itself to be billed as the "hookers' union." Where earlier reformers traded on outrage and pathos, COYOTE used humor and brought some sophistication to its dealings with the press.

Valerie Jenness offers a detailed analysis of COYOTE's discourse. COYOTE tried to redefine the terms of the debate over prostitution policy. While it had some early successes, its campiagn—like the movement to decriminalize marijuana—faded during the 1980s. Renamed the National Task Force on Prostitution, COYOTE endured, continuing to promote its cause but attracting less attention than it once had.

For sociologists, the case of COYOTE raises interesting questions. By presenting itself as a social movement of and for people labeled deviant, COYOTE violated expectations that social reform is the work of educated elites. And, by calling those deviant labels into question, COYOTE challenged the taken-for-granted construction of the prostitution problem and promoted radically different definitions of the market for sexual service. Operating at the intersection of deviance, gender, social problems, and social movements, COYOTE addressed issues which had implications extending far beyond prostitution policy. The fate of COYOTE's claims can teach us much about the processes by which social problems emerge and evolve.

Joel Best
Southern Illinois University
Carbondale

1

Introduction

A NEW VIEW OF PROSTITUTION

During the 1970s and throughout the 1980s a new image of prostitution emerged to challenge traditional views of prostitutes as social misfits, sexual slaves, victims of pimps and drug addiction, and tools of organized crime. It has become fashionable to refer to prostitution as "sex work" (du Plessix Gray 1992). This new image has been championed by the contemporary prostitutes' rights movement in the United States and abroad, which in turn has been led by the self-proclaimed prostitutes' rights organization COYOTE (an acronym for Call Off Your Old Tired Ethics). Since its emergence in the early 1970s, the prostitutes' rights movement has put forth vocal and persuasive leaders, while also gaining visibility in the mass media and the world of government grants, foundation support, the academy, social science disciplines, and nonprofit organizations.

The emergence of COYOTE and its movement to legitimate prostitution came as a surprise to both popular and scholarly observers. As one newspaper reporter explained:

> To me, the most interesting thing about COYOTE is that people who have been extremely put down by society are suddenly taking a superstrong position. . . . It's more than that. You're saying, "we aren't criminals, we are citizens, we demand so-and-so." It's like a social revolution from the bottom up. (Caruana 1974, p. 82)

On a more academic front, in his 1979 presidential address to the Society for the Study for Social Problems, Kitsuse observed: "Who would have thought that prostitutes would lobby the halls of legislative bodies to denounce 'your old tired ethics'?" (1980, p. 2).

Never before had prostitutes emerged to act as their own advocates by challenging commonly held notions about prostitution and offering proposals for reform. As Pheterson explained in *A Vindication of the Rights of Whores*:

> Never have prostitutes been legitimized as spokespersons or self-determining agents, not by those who defend them against male abuse and not by those who depend upon them for sexual service. It is a radical political stance to assume prostitute legitimacy. (1989, p. 3)

Insofar as it is fraught with difficulty, "to assume prostitute legitimacy" is a radical stance. In addition to confronting a dismal financial and cultural resource base, it is illegal for prostitutes to organize. To do so leaves them vulnerable to arrest for conspiracy and/or pimping and pandering. In essence, prostitutes' fear of being identified publicly and fear of reprisal from law enforcement hinders recruitment and visibility for a prostitutes' rights movement.

THE EMERGENCE OF A MOVEMENT

Although prostitution has existed in every society for which there are written records (Bullough and Bullough 1978; Lerner 1986; Murphy 1983; Otis 1985; Tannahill 1980), prostitutes' rights organizations are a fairly recent development in women's history, the history of sexual politics, and the history of prostitution. As Gagnon and Simon noted just prior to the formation of COYOTE, "there is no evidence that there has been internal organization among female prostitutes and the various occupational subcategories attached to this profession" (1973, p. 290). It is only since the early 1970s that prostitutes have organized to act as their own advocates.[1]

According to Hobson (1987), the prostitutes' rights movement was *officially* launched in Lyons, France in 1975 when local prostitutes took over a church and made public a list of grievances. At the heart of their strike was a plea to be protected from police harassment and repression that arose from a revision in French prostitution laws. In particular, this change resulted in prostitutes being forced to work on the streets, leaving them vulnerable to an increased number of physical assaults and arrests. This event in Lyons touched off a number of other events in France, all of which received unprecedented media attention. In the process, it raised public consciousness about the problems of prostitutes, while also giving rise to the formation and solidification of prostitutes' rights organizations in the United States and abroad.

Since the early 1970s, a number of prostitutes' rights organizations concerned with enhancing the welfare of prostitutes emerged in the United States. COYOTE is "the first and best-known of the prostitute groups" (Hobson 1987, p. 216). Despite a variety of obstacles, COYOTE quickly developed local branches in major cities across the United States. At the same time, many organizations emerged to serve as COYOTE's affiliates. Table 1.1 presents a listing of some these organizations.

Table 1.1. Prostitutes' Rights Organizations in the United States

ASP (Association of Seattle Prostitutes)
CAT (California Advocates for Trollops)
DOLPHIN (Dump Obsolete Laws; Prove Hypocrisy Isn't Necessary)
80s Ladies and Friends
FLOP (Friends and Lovers of Prostitutes)
HIRE (Hooking Is Real Employment)
Hooker's Hookup
HUM (Hooker's Union of Maryland)
NTFP (National Task Force on Prostitution)
PASSION (Professional Association Seeking Sexual Identification Observant of Nature)
PONY (Prostitutes of New York)
PUMA (Prostitutes' Union of Massachusetts Association)
SPARROW (Seattle Prostitutes against Rigid Rules over Women)

As prostitutes' rights organizations gained momentum in the United States throughout the 1970s and into the 1980s, so too did a number of them outside the United States' borders. COYOTE and its supporters have been primarily responsible for the formation of many of COYOTE's national and international affiliates, as well as the launching of an international campaign, by initiating and sustaining a network among these organizations. Table 1.2 lists some of COYOTE's international affiliates.

The organizations in Tables 1.1 and 1.2 act as the central voice in the prostitutes' rights movement currently under way in the United States and abroad.[2]

Table 1.2. Prostitutes' Rights Organizations Abroad

ICPR (International Committee for Prostitutes' Rights), Amsterdam
IPDC (International Prostitution Documentation Center), Geneva
PLAN (Prostitution Laws Are Nonsense), Great Britain
ECP (English Collective of Prostitutes), Great Britain
Comitato per i Diritti Civili delle Prostitute (Committee for the Civil Rights of Prostitutes), Italy
HYDRA, Berlin

(*continued*)

Table 1.2. (*Continued*)

HWG, Frankfurt
Solidarietaet Hamburger Huren (Solidarity of Hamburg Whores), Hamburg
Messalina, Munich
Kassandra, Nuremberg
Lysistrata, Cologne
Nitribitt, Bremen
CORP (Canadian Organization for Prostitutes)
Australian Prostitutes' Collective
Austrian Association of Prostitutes
De Rode Draad (The Red Thread), the Netherlands
De Roze Draad (The Pink Thread), the Netherlands
National Association of Prostitutes, Brazil

THE MESSAGE OF THE MOVEMENT

This book constitutes the first sustained effort to document the contemporary prostitutes' rights movement's twenty-year effort to enhance the status of prostitutes. The central goal of this movement has been to protect prostitutes from public designations of deviance, as well as from systems of legal and social control. In the process, the contemporary prostitutes' rights movement to legitimate prostitution has been greeted with ambivalence, support, criticism, and organized opposition.

The movement not only seeks to legitimate prostitution, but to celebrate it as well. It has developed a radical critique of popular views of prostitution by substituting a new ethic, one that affirms prostitutes' behavior as sensible and moral. In Kitsuse's (1980) terms, COYOTE represents an instance of deviants "coming out all over," not in acts of confession, but rather to profess and advocate the lives they live, along with the worth and values those lives express. Viewing themselves as a beleaguered minority group whose time to advocate reform has come, representatives and supporters of the prostitutes' rights movement reject the diagnosis of prostitutes' various conditions, as well as the attendant prescriptions for corrective treatment.

Throughout the history of the contemporary prostitutes' rights movement, COYOTE and its affiliates[3] have undertaken campaigns directed at a variety of concerns related to the status of prostitutes. By engaging in public debates, COYOTE's members have addressed such issues as discriminatory law enforcement practices (especially the entrapment and quarantining of prostitutes), the passage of the Equal Rights Amendment (ERA), violence against women (especially pornography and rape), the unconstitutionality of laws prohibiting prostitution, and a variety of concerns connected to the AIDS epidemic. Concerns such as these have provided a forum for COYOTE's crusade to legitimate the status of prostitutes and decriminalize prostitution.

The bulk of COYOTE's public activities have centered on creating and presenting various images of prostitutes that challenge depictions of prostitutes as social misfits, providers and victims of illicit sex, and "bad girls." To do this, COYOTE has been primarily concerned with dispelling the myth that prostitution is forced sexual slavery and that all prostitutes are necessarily victimized. At the heart of the contemporary prostitutes' rights movement are three interrelated claims. First, COYOTE and its supporters claim that not all prostitution is forced prostitution; in fact, they maintain that often prostitution is voluntarily chosen. Second, advocates argue that prostitution is legitimate service work and should be respected as such. Finally, COYOTE proclaims that to deny a woman the option to work as a prostitute, under conditions of her own choosing, is a violation of her civil rights.

Drawing on claims such as these, the movement to legitimate prostitution advocates the repeal of all existing prostitution laws, the reconstitution of prostitution as a viable service occupation, and the protection of prostitutes' civil rights as legitimate service workers. While acknowledging a number of abuses against women associated with prostitution (e.g., drug abuse among prostitutes, violence against prostitutes, and juvenile prostitution), COYOTE and its supporters claim that most of the problems associated with prostitution are directly related to the prohibition of prostitution, as well as the stigma attached to women, sex, and sex work. Moreover, from the point of view of COYOTE, forced prostitution and all the associated abuses against women cannot be addressed until voluntary prostitution is rendered legitimate.

Relying upon historical documents and public records, along with ethnographic and interview material, this book demonstrates that COYOTE has participated in three separate, albeit interrelated arenas of public debate over the last two decades. First, as a grass roots organization, COYOTE engaged local (i.e., San Francisco) law enforcement and municipal government officials in debate over selective and discriminatory enforcement of the criminal law. In the process, COYOTE leaders promoted an image of the prostitute as a victim of laws prohibiting prostitution rather than as a victim of illicit sex. Second, by participating in contemporary feminist debates on violence against women and the right of women to control and use their bodies as they see fit, COYOTE linked the problems of prostitutes to issues for women elsewhere in society. In so doing, the prostitutes' rights movement gained national attention and found an institutionalized forum for pressing its claims about prostitution as voluntarily chosen service work. Finally, as the AIDS epidemic reached alarming proportions, prostitutes' rights organizations emerged as watchdog organizations to counter assertions that prostitutes were spreading the disease, thus forging a link between public health agencies and sex workers.

By engaging in these three arenas of debate, the prostitutes' rights movement has ongoingly threatened to take "ownership" (Gusfield 1975) of the problem of prostitution away from traditional experts. It has done so by participating in public arenas of discourse that parallel those that have historically been intimately connected to both the construction of prostitution as a social problem and the defining of prostitutes as deviants. Specifically, throughout the nineteenth and twentieth centuries, prostitution has been defined as problematic and prostitutes construed as deviants by three basic constituencies: (1) law enforcement agencies, (2) moral entrepreneurs and social crusaders (including nineteenth-century feminists), and (3) public health officials. Not coincidentally then, COYOTE has anchored its contemporary crusade in debates with adversarial representatives of each of these constituencies.

Drawing on a detailed empirical record, the analysis in this book details how public debate in each of these arenas has made distinct contributions to the growth and direction of the prostitutes' rights movement. By extension, I examine how the movement has contributed to public discourse surrounding prostitution as a social problem and prostitutes as deviants. The central argument is that COYOTE and its supporters have managed to reshape the symbolic landscape surrounding prostitution as a social problem by promoting prostitution as a legitimate women's and civil rights issue. Specifically, by invoking and institutionalizing a vocabulary of sex as work, prostitutes as sex workers, and prostitutes' civil rights as workers, the contemporary prostitutes' rights movement serves to sever the social problem of prostitution from its historical association with crime and illicit sex, and place it firmly in the rhetoric of work, choice, and civil rights. In effect, what has been construed as a sin in the past and criminal today is currently being fought over as possibly credible in the future. As Gusfield argues, "the 'lifting' of a deviant activity to the level of a political, public issue is a sign that its moral passage is at stake" (1967, p. 188).

THEORETICAL FRAMING

Theoretically speaking, this work focuses on how such "lifting" occurs, especially when initiated and undertaken by representatives of a disenfranchised and highly stigmatized constituency. For the purposes of this book, I conceptualize COYOTE and its affiliates as social movement organizations vying for control of the definition of a social problem that is highly associated with deviance and social control. Clearly, the contemporary prostitutes' rights movement is a moral crusade shrouded in layers of stigma. In view of the deeply ingrained historically negative views of prostitution (Bergman 1988; Brandt 1987; D'Emilio and Freedman 1988; Murphy 1983; Otis 1985), the movement has existed in an environment that is hostile toward its members, constituents, and goals.

In light of this, over the last twenty years the prostitutes' rights movement has undertaken what one reporter has referred to as "one massive public relations project" (Eric Sorensen, personal interview, June 3, 1992) in an effort to reconstitute the problem of prostitution and normalize the work of prostitutes. Since prostitution has never been accepted as a legitimate activity, much less a professional or occupational one, COYOTE has sought to make its unpopular philosophy more palatable, its constituency more honorable, and its cause more acceptable. In the process, COYOTE's representatives have had to devote inordinate attention to establishing and maintaining legitimacy as a resource for their crusade. Assuming that legitimation is a primary resource for organizations in general and social movement organizations in particular, this work focuses on how COYOTE and its affiliates manage the acquisition, establishment, and loss of legitimacy. In short, how does the movement operate in the shadows of ill repute while trying to diminish those shadows?

By framing the contemporary prostitutes' rights movement as a small but vocal movement emerging from the "lunatic fringe" (DeYoung 1984), this book ultimately moves beyond documenting the contemporary prostitutes' rights movement to question if and how social movements associated with deviance and deviants operate differently from those undertaken by what Goffman (1963) refers to as "normals." Social movements undertaken by or representing constituencies embedded in layers of stigma certainly confront mobilization dilemmas similar to those of other social movements. However, they also confront added dilemmas. Most notable, so-called "immoral crusades" must establish and maintain legitimacy while operating in a cultural "yoke of disreputability" (Weitzer 1991). But how is this accomplished? And, more specifically, what types of transformations must the movement, as well as the source(s) of the imputations of deviance, undergo in the process?

In order to approach these types of concerns, this work is anchored in one of the dominant sociological frameworks of the last few decades, namely, the constructionist approach to social problems as definitional activities (Best 1987, 1990; Gusfield 1963, 1967, 1968, 1981, 1984; Kitsuse 1980; Schneider 1978, 1984, 1985; Schneider and Kitsuse 1984; Spector 1977, 1981; Spector and Kitsuse 1973, 1977). Gusfield has noted that the constructionist approach "has gone under many names and in many directions: ethnomethodology, phenomenology, various kinds of structuralism, hermeneutics, cognitive sociology, and symbolic interaction" (1984, p. 37). What all of these approaches have in common, however, is a focus on the processes by which subject matter is constructed by human actors (Collins 1981; Giddens 1976).

Central to this tradition is a focus on the full range of definitional activities that describe and ultimately reconstruct social problems, and by extension the deviance associated with such problems. From this perspective, rather than studying the "objective" conditions that are deemed social problems, the focus is on how such conditions have been defined through interpretive procedures and collective action. The phrase *interpretive procedures* refers to activities through which meanings are attached to phenomena such that the phenomena are construed, and ultimately understood, in particular ways (e.g., as problematic or deviant).

Emanating from the symbolic interactionist tradition (Blumer 1969, 1971), the constructionist approach to understanding definitional processes focuses on claims-making activities in particular (Altheide and Johnson 1980; Aronson 1982, 1984; Best 1987, 1990; Fishman 1978; Schneider 1985). As Spector and Kitsuse have noted, claims-making is "the activities of individuals or groups making grievances and claims with respect to some putative conditions" (1977, p. 75). As such, claims-making activities are a primary mechanism through which social movements are incited, the moral order is negotiated, and social problems are constructed.

COYOTE provides a fertile ground for the examination of collective action, definitional processes, interpretive procedures, and claims-making activities. Clearly, the prostitutes' rights movement qualifies as a moral crusade advocating various reform; after all, it has emerged to put forth grievances and claims that "certain conditions are intolerable and must be changed" (Spector and Kitsuse 1977, p. 148). In essence, COYOTE and its affiliates are claims-making social movement organizations that defend the rights of prostitutes, who are portrayed as having been "wronged" in a multitude of ways by representatives from numerous adversarial constituencies.

COYOTE AS THE EMPIRICAL FOCUS

In order to approach the empirical and theoretical concerns identified above, I have made COYOTE the focus of this work for three reasons. First, it is the organization at the hub of the prostitutes' rights movement. COYOTE not only began the movement in the United States, but it continues to anchor it as well. As the most consistently active, it remains the most visible of the prostitutes' rights organizations in the United States.

The second reason is that it advocates the most controversial, and some would say extreme, position on prostitutes' rights in contemporary sexual politics. COYOTE's position on prostitution flies in the face of dominant feminist analyses of prostitution (Overall 1992), historically developed conceptions of prostitution, and media-produced images of prostitutes (Schur 1984). In essence, the very substance of COYOTE's position creates obstacles and constraints for the organizations' members, supporters, and movement to legitimate prostitution.

Finally, COYOTE constitutes the empirical anchoring point of this work because, unlike other prostitutes' rights organizations, it has managed to survive and proliferate since its inception. Despite the obstacles COYOTE faced in its formative years, it has grown into a national and then an international organization. Moreover, COYOTE has maintained a lengthy and well-documented history, which is crucial when one undertakes research of this type.

DATA DESCRIPTION AND METHOD OF ANALYSIS

Few organizations have commissioned or attempted detailed and/or systematic histories of their routine work, policies, personnel, and operations. In this regard, COYOTE is no exception. Thus, to carry out this research I relied upon the proverbial "next best thing." This work is primarily based on historical documents housed in the archives of the Schlesinger Library at Radcliffe College in Cambridge, Massachusetts. These holdings are stored in thirty-five cartons, two and a half file boxes, and a variety of folders and folios. The library also stores information related to the prostitutes' rights movement on four videotapes, one phonograph record, and one audio cassette.

As COYOTE's organizational records, these documents were donated to the Schlesinger Library in 1981, 1982, and 1984 by Margo St. James, the founder of COYOTE. Although St. James submitted documents to the library at three different times, the information contained spans the years from 1973 to 1984. These holdings are officially closed to the public until the death of St. James. However, authorization from St. James, coupled with cooperation from the staff of the Schlesinger Library, enabled me to gain access to the documents. I reviewed and photocopied thousands of documents from these holdings, including prostitutes' rights organizations' newsletters (e.g., *COYOTE Howls*), interviews with organizational members and critics, meeting minutes and notes, questionnaires and reports, position statements, public and personal correspondence, resolutions, grant abstracts and proposals, membership lists, newspaper clippings reporting on COYOTE's activities, telephone logs, budgets, contracts, news releases, conference agendas and charters, and videotapes of four nationally syndicated talk shows in which COYOTE representatives appeared as guests.

To supplement the materials housed at the Schlesinger Library, I also relied upon COYOTE's more recent organizational records. Priscilla Alexander, the former codirector of COYOTE and the former executive director of the National Task Force on Prostitution, allowed me to review and photocopy material in her San Francisco office.[4] These materials, which are dated 1985–1990, allowed me to document COYOTE's more recent activities.

In addition to the material obtained from the Schlesinger Library and from COYOTE's main office in San Francisco, I have interviewed and remained in contact with St. James and Alexander. Both of them have facilitated this work by providing me with interviews, documents, and other information that has allowed me to keep current with the activities of the prostitutes' rights movement. Contact with St. James and Alexander has also allowed me to capture the leaders' perspective on the organization, its crusade, and its future.

Finally, I employed a variety of supplementary materials containing information on COYOTE and its affiliates and/or the prostitutes' rights movement. Included in these sources are published texts that report on or address the movement, as well as a variety of newsletters published by prostitutes' rights organizations.[5]

The materials described above constitute a unique and irreplaceable source of data for this research in at least two ways. First, when combined they provided me with an empirical record of COYOTE's historical and contemporary activities, including COYOTE's place and participation in the prostitutes' rights movement. Second, they provided me with empirical evidence of COYOTE's ideology and political strategies, as well as its role in attempting to reshape public perceptions of women, sex, sexuality, and prostitution. In essence, when combined these materials allowed me first and foremost to render visible what has heretofore, at least from a scholarly point of view, been an ignored organization and social movement.[6]

Consistent with the theoretical framework supporting this work, I viewed the historical data used for this research as the remnants of the work and activity of COYOTE's leaders, members, and supporters (Bittner 1965; Zimmerman and Pollner 1970). Thus, I presume they bear the marks and reflect the agendas, as well as foibles, mistakes, vagaries, and inconsistencies of such work. In short, I approached these as the by-products of interested actors playing important roles in the definitional process.

Despite traditional prejudices against using case studies in social science, in this work I do just that for a variety of reasons. First, although case studies can rely upon a variety of research methods (Becker 1968; Broomley 1986; Jacob 1987; Kennedy 1979; Owens 1982; Stake 1978; Yin 1984), they are nonetheless a preferred strategy when 'how' and 'why' questions are being posed. This is especially true when the investigator has little control over the phenomena being studied and when the empirical focus is on contemporary phenomena within some real-life context (Yin 1981a, 1981b), which is the case with this and all social movements. Second, like other methods of research, case studies allow for exploration, description, *and* theory building. Third, case study approaches allow for the incorporation of multiple sources of evidence (i.e., public and private documents, interviews, and observations), which is what I do throughout this effort. Finally, and most importantly, a case study approach allowed for the sketching of the prostitutes' rights movement over time with a sensitivity to the sociopolitical context within which COYOTE's crusade has developed, and from which it cannot be separated.

By employing a case study approach, I pursued two objectives. The first was to empirically document and ultimately describe COYOTE's social movement. In the process of simply describing the contemporary prostitutes' rights movement, I pursued an answer to the question What is it? rather than How does it work? At this stage, the initial goal was to offer an historical description that is more comprehensive, more meaningful, and more useful than those in common currency, especially in the scholarly literature. My second objective was to make analytic sense of the evolution of the contemporary prostitutes' rights movement. Thus, the analysis in the following chapters includes an examination of the properties of the claims put forth by COYOTE, how these claims have been received by both hostile and supportive constituencies, and how COYOTE's crusade has been shaped over time. In the process, the following types of questions were pursued: What is the definition of the "problem" of prostitution and prostitutes according to COYOTE? What prescriptions for solution(s) does COYOTE offer? How are such prescriptions disseminated to the public in general and relevant constituencies in particular? And how does COYOTE's message get shaped in attempts to increase the movement's viability, as well as the message's acceptability?

With regard to the latter question, and commensurate with the theoretical framework adopted in this effort, my analytic goal was to examine the viability, rather than the validity, of COYOTE's claims. I understood viable claims as definitions and assertions that "live" and that claimants could "get away with" (Spector and Kitsuse 1977). Viability was evident when prostitutes and their advocates, critics, and constituencies gave credibility to claims and definitions by responding to them and/or by offering counterclaims. In short, I did not pursue the study of COYOTE and its affiliates for what it could reveal about the conduct of prostitutes or the conditions of prostitution in a factual sense. Rather, this work was pursued for what it can reveal about the reconstruction of a social problem and the normalization of deviance.

OVERVIEW OF THE BOOK

Having introduced the contemporary prostitutes' rights movement, framed it in a sociologically meaningful way, and briefly described the data and method of analysis employed in this work, this chapter concludes with an overview of the remaining chapters.

In Chapter 2 I document the larger historical and political context that preceded and coincided with the contemporary prostitutes' rights movement. In order to accomplish this, I discuss the social movements and discursive themes that provided the sociopolitical milieu that fueled the contemporary prostitutes' rights movement. Specifically, I examine contemporary discourse on victimless crimes, sex law reform, sexual civil liberties, women's right to control their bodies, and violence against women. This examination is designed to place the contemporary prostitutes' rights movement in an historical context and to demonstrate that public discussions surrounding other issues and their attendant social movements provided the crucible for the emergence of the contemporary prostitutes' rights movement, as well as an ongoing cultural resource for prostitutes' rights organizations.

In Chapter 3 I describe COYOTE as a San Francisco–based grass roots organization engaging in debates with local law enforcement and government officials. In the process, I delineate the way in which COYOTE's early campaign gained support from prostitutes, reform-minded liberals, and other organizations by projecting a new image of prostitutes. This new image promoted the prostitute as a victim of laws prohibiting prostitution and the discriminatory enforcement of such laws, rather than as a victim of illicit sex and the commodification of women. In short, this chapter details how COYOTE's early campaign capitalized on San Francisco's "culture of civility" (Becker and Horowitz 1971) to suggest that it is a waste of taxpayers' money to enforce laws that simply create and perpetuate, rather than eliminate the victimization of women (i.e., of prostitutes).

Throughout Chapter 4 I examine how the prostitutes' rights movement's participation in feminist discourse facilitated a crystallization of COYOTE's views, gained national attention, and found an institutionalized forum for pressing their claims about prostitution. Moreover, I chronicle how coalition building and the development of ties with the contemporary women's movement allowed the prostitutes' rights movement to reach beyond the technical aspects of enforcement of criminal laws governing prostitution. Within the parameters of the women's movement, especially the discourse on violence against women, the prostitutes' rights movement was able to press claims about prostitution as a women's issue and as voluntarily chosen service work.

Chapter 5 brings the contemporary prostitutes' rights movement up to date by analyzing the way in which the AIDS epidemic has affected its evolution. I demonstrate that the AIDS epidemic is a dual-edged sword for prostitutes' rights organizations. It has supplied resources to them, while also siphoning personnel from them and circumventing their original goal to decriminalize prostitution. In brief, this chapter demonstrates that COYOTE and its affiliates have emerged as watchdog organizations primarily concerned with countering assertions that prostitutes represent "pools of contagion" and threatening avenues of transmission for the AIDS epidemic. Accordingly, this chapter focuses on how the prostitutes' rights movement has undertaken a defensive campaign to protest the scapegoating of prostitutes for AIDS, while also forging a link between public health agencies and sex workers.

Borrowing from the findings in previous chapters, in Chapter 6 I describe the primary strategies by which members of COYOTE have pursued the acquisition of legitimacy as a primary resource for the institutionalization of their cause. These strategies include establishing the organization in an environment supportive of deviant activities and organizations, placing the plea to decriminalize prostitution in acceptable political discourse, building coalitions with established organizations and social causes, capitalizing on the AIDS epidemic as an environmental crisis, and institutionalizing the claim that COYOTE is an organization *of and for* working prostitutes. Ultimately, in this chapter I suggest that strategies such as these serve to disclaim COYOTE's deviant status, as well as the organization's illegitimacy.

In the final chapter of this book, I briefly summarize the empirical findings of this research as a precursor to discussing the theoretical implications born of the empirical effort. By drawing on the analyses presented in the previous chapters, I offer a theoretical discussion that focuses on social processes underlying the efforts of COYOTE and its affiliates to compete in a highly competitive "social problems marketplace" (Best 1990, p. 15). More specifically, my theoretical focus is on social processes surrounding the prostitutes' rights movement's efforts to *re*constitute prostitution as a social problem, including the establishment of arenas of debate, the pursuit of "frame alignment" (Snow and Benford 1988; Snow, Rochford, Worden, and Benford 1986), and the disavowal of deviance. With a consideration of these processes in mind, this book concludes with a formulation of a "natural history of *re*constructed social problems" model.

NOTES

1. Individuals and organizations have fought for the rights of prostitutes throughout the last two centuries. For example, activist Josephine Butler began fighting for prostitutes' rights in the mid–nineteenth century when she fought for the repeal of the Contagious Diseases Acts (Jaget 1980). More recently, throughout the 1970s and into the 1980s, the American Civil Liberties Union (ACLU) has been working on the prostitution issue as part of its Sexual Privacy Project.

2. These lists are by no means exhaustive, nor do they necessarily reflect organizations that are alive and well at present. Prostitutes' rights organizations can emerge and die quite quickly, depending upon local conditions and contingencies. Moreover, these organizations' level of active involvement in the prostitutes' rights movement has waxed and waned historically.

3. Throughout this book, in stating positions, analyses, claims, or campaigns, I mean to imply COYOTE taken together with all of its affiliates. However, I will simply say "COYOTE."

4. In 1986 St. James moved to France to work through the International Committee for Prostitutes' Rights (ICPR) and Alexander, who had been working with St. James in San Francisco, became the leader of COYOTE. A more thorough discussion of this shift in leadership is presented in Chapter 5.

5. For example, I relied upon: *Female Sexual Slavery* (1979), by Kathleen Barry; *Good Girls/Bad Girls: Feminists and Sex Trade Workers Face to Face* (1987), edited by Laurie Bell; *Sex Work: Writings by Women in the Sex Industry* (1987), edited by Frederique Delacoste and Priscilla Alexander; *Working: My Life as a Prostitute* (1988), by Dolores French (with Linda Lee); *A Vindication of the Rights of Whores* (1989), edited by Gail Pheterson; *The Whore Stigma: Female Dishonor and Male Unworthiness* (1986), by Gail Pheterson; *Horizontal,* an Austria-based prostitutes' newsletter; *The Oldest Profession Times*, a Sacramento-based prostitutes' newsletter; *WHISPER* (Women Hurt in Systems of Oppression Engaged in Revolt), a New York–based newsletter; and *World Wide Whore's News* (WWWN), an international prostitutes' rights newsletter.

6. The only exception to this is Weitzer's (1991) article, "Prostitutes' Rights in the United States," which was published in *Sociological Quarterly*.

2

Contemporary Sexual Politics: Setting the Stage for the Contemporary Prostitutes' Rights Movement and a New Discourse on Prostitution

INTRODUCTION

As Foucault recognized, "for centuries now, the discourse on sex has been multiplied rather than rarified" (1980, p. 53). Over the past thirty years in particular, beliefs about sexuality and the social control of sex have been challenged, altered, and often undermined. In the process, sexuality, in the broadest sense of the word, has increasingly moved from the private sphere into the center of public debates (D'Emilio and Freedman 1988; Rubin 1984; Seidman 1992; Weeks 1985). As Weeks concluded in *Sexuality and Its Discontents*:

> There has been an unprecedented mobilisation of political forces around sexual issues. A hundred years ago the possibility of a sexual politics was virtually unthinkable. Today it is commonplace on [the] Right and Left. . . . Sex has become a potent political issue because of a perplexing and seemingly endless conflict of beliefs as to the appropriate ways of living our sexualities. (1985, p. 16)

As a result of such conflicts, the politics of sexuality have increasingly constituted core political issues.

In the last quarter of a century in particular, significant social movements have emerged to create a new era of sexual politics. Occupying center stage in the play of contemporary sexual politics have been movements to decriminalize victimless crimes, the gay and lesbian movement, the women's movement, and the emergent New Right. Largely as a result of the public debate inspired by these movements, questions of individual and public harm, choice and consent, and constitutional rights have increasingly come to characterize contemporary public discourse on sex and all that surrounds it.

Historically speaking, the prostitutes' rights movement has ridden on the coattails of the liberal movements of the 1960s and the 1970s, while also being confronted with the conservative backlash of the New Right in the late 1970s and throughout the 1980s. The discursive themes emanating from the "rights" movements of the 1960s and 1970s formed the sociopolitical terrain that inspired and fueled the contemporary prostitutes' rights movement, while the conservative politics of the 1980s presented obstacles for the movement. Ultimately, however, the contemporary prostitutes' rights movement capitalized upon the dissemination of discourse from each of these social movements and their attendant arenas of debate to frame its grievances, press its claims, and seek support for the movement.

Since its inception, the movement has adopted rhetoric consistent with the discursive landscape created by prior and coinciding social movements concerned with sexuality (broadly construed) and the law. Although it is beyond the scope of this chapter to provide a comprehensive analysis of historical and contemporary sexual politics, it is sufficient to briefly recall the trend toward decriminalizing victimless crimes, the debates over the expansion of sexual civil liberties to sexual minorities, and contemporary efforts to challenge the sexual double standard by pursuing equality for women. The salience of these core issues is made most transparent through an examination of the contemporary movement to decriminalize victimless crimes, the gay and lesbian movement, the contemporary women's movement, current debates on pornography and violence against women, contemporary discourse on prostitution, and the campaign(s) of the New Right. I discuss each of these organized efforts in order to demonstrate the way in which their attendant discourse merges to publicly question sexual and legal matters connected to concerns with public and personal harm, constitutional rights, and consent.[1] It is the proliferation of this discourse that serves as a political backdrop, as well as a rhetorical resource, for COYOTE's crusade to enhance the status of prostitutes.

CONCEPTUALIZING VICTIMLESS CRIMES

Historically, there have been disputes over whether certain behaviors and activities, such as prostitution, should be considered sins, vices, diseases, or simply matters of personal choice (Goode and Troiden 1974; Hyde 1982; Schur 1965). These activities and behaviors have been defined and commonly understood as victimless crimes. Like prostitution, activities such as suicide, gambling, and drug use have fallen under the purview of the law through victimless-crime statutes.

Sex law is one of the most visible instruments of sexual regulation and sexual stratification. Attempts to control sexual activities have been pursued through the establishment of statutes dealing with fornication, cohabitation, adultery, miscegenation, homosexuality, and most importantly for the purposes of this work, prostitution.[2] What these sex-related activities share is a status as victimless crimes in jurisdictions across the United States. The legal regulation of these activities has historically taken place by criminalizing specific forms of sexual behavior.

Regardless of which definition of victimless crime one chooses, the core of any definition contains some combination of an exchange transaction, the lack of apparent harm to others, and the absence of a complainant (Hughes 1975; Hyde 1982; Jones, Gallagher, and McFalls 1988; Morris and Hawkins 1970; Packer 1968; Schur 1965). As Schur noted, the "element of consent precludes the existence of a victim—in the usual sense of the word" (1965, p. v). Victimless crimes, especially those related to sexual activity, most often occur in situations wherein one person obtains from another a commodity or personal service that is socially disapproved and legally proscribed. This is done in a fairly direct manner where all parties concerned not only desire to avoid the restriction imposed by the related statute, but consent to the behavior as well.

Because of the ambiguous and debatable nature of consent and harm associated with victimless crimes, the victim in such crimes is at best elusive and often absent. In a victimless crime, who constitutes the victim is open to debate, moral judgment, and contemporary politics. Accordingly, historically there has been a range of views on how much individual and/or public harm is associated with the behavior or activity in question, as well as the degree of consent involved in the activity.

In victimless crimes, the law specifies or implies that individuals are the victims of their own behavior(s). That is, individuals are simultaneously identified as perpetrators and as victims. For example, antihomosexuality and antiprostitution statutes have, at least in part, been aimed at preventing harm to homosexuals and prostitutes through these activities. This attribution of victimization is independent of the individual's self-identification as a victim; in fact, attributions of harm are often made in spite of the perpetrator/victim's pronouncements of consent and lack of harm. It is this situation that epitomizes a central point of contention among various factions in contemporary sexual politics in general and between representatives of the prostitutes' rights movement and their critics in particular.

Beyond protecting specific perpetrators from their own behavior, victimless-crime statutes involve attempts to legislate morality for its own sake. Statutes surrounding victimless crimes are aimed at protecting society in general. Thus, they are often described as "crimes against nature," "crimes against the state," or "crimes against morals." In the case of homosexuality and prostitution, victimless crime statutes are aimed at protecting the "population at large" from the perceived negative effects of same-sex activity and sex for sale.

For the purposes of this work, two points are central to understanding victimless crimes. First, the introduction and enforcement of statutes resulting in the creation of these crimes is anchored in attributions of individual and societal harm. Victimless-crime statutes are justified insofar as they can be said to protect individuals and society from harmful activities. Second, the attributions of harm associated with victimless crimes are not fixed. The perception of harm related to sexual matters in particular is negotiable. It is historically variable and open to political waves and dominant ideologies, which becomes apparent through an examination of the movement to decriminalize victimless crimes.

MOVEMENT TO DECRIMINALIZE VICTIMLESS CRIMES

One of the most notable legal trends since the 1960s and into the 1980s has been a movement to decriminalize victimless crimes, especially those surrounding sexuality and sexual conduct (Hyde 1982; Mueller 1980). Based on a "no harm, no foul" ideology, a liberalization of sex-related laws has come into play chiefly in attacks on sex laws through the courts (Boggan, Haft, Lister, and Ripp 1975; Brent 1976). That is, in the past two decades a great deal of legislative change surrounding the status of sex-related victimless crimes has been proposed, contested, and adopted.

Legal changes have been primarily based on the assertion that when an act does no harm to anyone, and provides neither a victim nor a complainant, then it cannot reasonably be defined as a crime (Hughes 1975; Hyde 1982; Mueller 1980; Schur 1965). Through arguments suggesting that particular behaviors defined as criminal are freely chosen and consensual, and fail to be associated with individual and/or public harm, many victimless-crime statutes have been questioned and subsequently eradicated.

Challenges to these statutes have also been based on cost effectiveness analyses. The thrust of this argument was articulated by Norval Morris of the University of Chicago Law School:

> Most of our legislation concerning drunkenness, narcotics, gambling, and sexual behavior is wholly misguided. It is based on an exaggerated conception of the capacity of the criminal law to influ-

> ence men and, ironically, on a simultaneous belief in the limited capacity of men to govern themselves. We incur enormous collateral costs for that exaggeration and we overload our criminal justice system to a degree that renders it grossly defective where we really need protection—from violence and depredations on our property. (1973, p. 11)

Arguments such as this appeal not only to the public's sense of the degree of harm resulting from victimless crimes, but to its pocketbooks as well. With regard to prostitution, it is this type of logic that COYOTE has relied heavily upon when debating with law enforcement officials. As described in Chapter 3, COYOTE has contested law enforcement's categorization of prostitution as a victimless crime by basing its arguments in a simultaneous denial of the victimization associated with sex for sale and the economic inefficiency of enforcing prostitution-related statutes.

Of course, such appeals have not gone uncontested, especially in the last ten years. Critics of the movement to decriminalize victimless crimes have historically argued that the decriminalization of behaviors associated with these crimes only results in the proliferation of immoral behavior and the adoption of morally abhorrent life-styles. Such behaviors and life-styles, so the argument goes, are not only harmful to the implicated individual(s), they also necessarily lead to the moral decay of society. In the mid- to late 1970s and throughout the 1980s, the constituencies commonly referred to as the New Right have been most publicly responsible for advocating an antidecriminalization position on victimless crimes, including prostitution.

LEGAL PRINCIPLES IN SEX LAW REFORM

In addition to promoting the decriminalization of sex-related victimless crimes by invoking a "no harm, no foul" vocabulary and a cost-*in*effectiveness analysis, political struggles to contest restrictions on sexual activities, including prostitution, have centered on a discourse of rights. Appeals to constitutional rights and to the expansion of civil liberties have loomed large in campaigns to remove sex-related victimless-crime statutes, and to grant minorities privileges equivalent to those of majorities. Two important legal principles in particular have consistently been used to bring about changes in sex-related statutes: the constitutional right to privacy and the constitutional right to free expression. Under the rubric of these two principles, laws restricting sexual behavior have been attacked, and continue to be attacked, as attempts to legislate private morality in a manner that violates individuals' constitutional rights.

Specifically, the contemporary gay and lesbian movement and the contemporary women's movement have emerged to claim their constituencies' "rights."[3] The gay and lesbian movement has relied heavily upon the constitutional right to privacy in the pursuit of sexual and affectional equality for gays and lesbians. Similarly, the contemporary women's movement has relied heavily upon the constitutional right to privacy in the pursuit of women's right to abortion in particular and their right to control their bodies more generally. In Chapters 3 and 4 I document how COYOTE borrowed heavily from the discourse emanating from each of these movements to claim prostitutes' constitutional right to engage in consensual, harmless, sex. As the codirector of COYOTE informed me in correspondence:

> Margo and I had a combination of libertarian and socialist world concepts that helped to focus our analysis over the years. We are also beholden to the work of the lesbian/gay rights movement, the women's movement, and the work of radical historians. (Priscilla Alexander, personal communication, February 22, 1990)

Clearly, the gay and lesbian movement and the contemporary women's movement have contributed greatly to the discourse of contemporary sexual politics. Specifically, each of these movements, like the contemporary prostitutes' rights movement, constitutes an arena wherein issues of harm, consent, and constitutional rights have been ongoingly negotiated.

THE GAY AND LESBIAN MOVEMENT

Although the founding of the Mattachine Society in 1950 and that of the Daughters of Bilitis in 1955 are often cited as the first signs of a gay and lesbian movement, it was not until the late 1960s that gay men and lesbians became politically mobilized to fight discrimination and repeal antihomosexuality laws (Adam 1979, 1989; D'Emilio and Freedman 1988; Stivision 1982; Weeks 1985). The struggle against homophobic discrimination has been fought on many levels. The initial intent of the early gay and lesbian movement was to disrupt stereotypic perceptions of homosexuality as a peculiar condition (Adam 1989; Katz 1976; Weeks 1985). Since then, it has continually sought to establish homosexuality as a nonstigmatized public alternative to heterosexual standards.

Throughout the history of the gay and lesbian movement, legal redress has been at the core of its political activities (Adam 1989; Stivison

1982). The struggle has been between gay and lesbian advocates and those who oppose granting homosexuals full civil liberties. In 1967 the ACLU took up the issue of discrimination against homosexuals by relying upon the constitutional right to privacy. The ACLU continues to challenge government regulation of private consensual sexual behavior on the grounds that it infringes upon individuals' constitutional right to privacy (D'Emilio 1983; Stivison 1982).

Many proposals on behalf of homosexuals to alter or eradicate state and national legislation have been put forth since the 1960s (Leonard 1992). For example, gay and lesbian advocates have proposed to amend the 1964 Civil Rights Act by also prohibiting discrimination based on "affectional or sexual preference." However, in 1976 and again in 1986 the Supreme Court upheld the constitutionality of state antihomosexual laws. More recently, lesbian and gay advocates have lobbied for the removal of military regulations that make homosexual acts grounds for dishonorable discharge, denial of military benefits, and/or court-martial. Regardless of the particular issue at hand, representatives of the gay and lesbian movement have continually opposed the law's interference with what is construed as basically a victimless activity that is avidly sought and mutually agreed upon. Moreover, the gay and lesbian movement has pursued the expansion of sexual civil liberties by emphasizing the private and consensual nature of homosexual acts and life-styles and by continually repudiating the harm associated with homosexual behaviors and life-styles in particular and sexual deviance in general (Adam 1989; Altman 1971, 1982; D'Emilio 1983; Katz 1976; Marotta 1981).

Some states have liberalized laws concerning homosexuality by eliminating penalties against private sexual relationships, both homosexual and heterosexual, between consenting adults. According to some analysts, there has been an increased tolerance toward gays and lesbians, in large part because of the gay and lesbian movement and the general liberalization of the last few decades (Adam 1989; Altman 1971; Goode and Troiden 1974; Jones et al. 1988; Katz 1976; Rubin 1984; Weeks 1985).

Regardless of the future of the gay and lesbian movement, its presence has served to fundamentally shape the discourse of contemporary sexual politics. In essence, the gay and lesbian movement helped create a sociopolitical climate more hospitable to prostitutes and their advocates. Not surprisingly, and as the next chapter details, the discursive themes of the gay and lesbian movement have been adopted by the prostitutes' rights movement. Similarly, the themes emanating from the contemporary women's movement have proved instrumental in launching the prostitutes' rights movement, as well as defusing it.

THE CONTEMPORARY WOMEN'S MOVEMENT

Although the contemporary women's movement addresses a broad set of concerns, sexuality and the social control of sex have certainly dominated its agenda (D'Emilio and Freedman 1988; Ferree and Hess 1985; Snitow, Stansell and Thompson 1983; Weeks 1985). The development of modern feminist sexual politics has been a complex process, whose full history has yet to be told. But, "as the sexuality debate goes, so goes feminism" (Ellis quoted in Weeks 1985, p. 218).

In the widely cited *Second Sex* (1953), Simone de Beauvoir influenced an entire generation of women by insisting that sexual autonomy is fundamental to the pursuit of women's liberation. By contrast, in *The Feminine Mystique* (1963), Betty Friedan warned that issues of sexuality were only distractions from the pursuit of women's liberation, and as such the emphasis on sexual politics is dangerous and misguided. Instead of focusing on the achievement of sexual autonomy, Friedan urged women to focus on locating and securing meaningful work. De Beauvoir's affirmations of sexuality and Friedan's cautions about sexuality set the initial stage for tension in the women's movement over the place of sex in the struggle to liberate women. As Rubin succinctly remarked:

> Feminism has always been vitally interested in sex. But there has [*sic*] been two strains of feminist thought on the subject. One tendency has criticized the restrictions on women's sexual behavior and denounced the high cost imposed on women for being sexually active. This feminist tradition of sexual thought has called for a sexual liberation that would work for women as well as for men. The second tendency has considered sexual liberalization to be an inherently male extension of male privilege. (1984, p. 301)

While sex and its multitude of manifestations have simultaneously been perceived as a potentially liberating force and a source of women's oppression, feminists advanced multiple stances toward postwar sexual trends (Seidman 1992).

Abortion

Throughout the late 1960s and into the 1970s the belief that women's sexual autonomy and freedom was a prerequisite for women's liberation was affirmed across a variety of constituencies (D'Emilio and Freedman 1988; Ferree and Hess 1985; Firestone 1970; Millet 1970; Snitow et al. 1983). The growing conviction that women had the *right* to be sexual without the consequences of pregnancy made abortion an immediate concern that has dominated discussions and political strategies for feminists for decades. Indeed, one of the major political struggles for the women's movement continues to be the fight to eliminate laws restricting abortion (Deckard 1975; Ferree and Hess 1985; Mansbridge 1986; Snitow et al. 1983).

Feminists' fight for reproductive rights, especially access to legal abortions, has historically been packaged as a struggle for women's absolute right to control and use their bodies as they see fit. In general, this right has been viewed as a necessary prerequisite for women's sexual freedom and self-determination. Women's right to control their bodies has encompassed everything from the right to refuse sex to the right to a freely chosen sexuality. In short, the insistence on women's right to self-determination is the foundation of the feminist position.

Feminists have fought long and hard to establish and secure women's right to choose to have an abortion, and to ensure public funding to make it possible for all women to exercise that choice. In 1973 the women's movement's struggle to achieve abortion on demand won a major victory. In *Roe v. Wade,* the Supreme Court decided that state laws forbidding abortion violated women's right to privacy implicit in the Constitution's Fourth Amendment. That is, the Supreme Court affirmed that a woman's constitutional right to privacy extended to the right to have an abortion.

Since *Roe v. Wade,* many attacks have been made, and continue to be made, on women's right to abortion. Both prochoice and antiabortion advocates have relied upon a language of constitutional rights to press their claims. Prochoice advocates argue that the constitutional right to privacy should extend to women's right to choose to have abortions, while also having access to safe abortions. At the same time, prolife activists construe the abortion issue as an abstract moral issue having solely to do with the rights of the unborn fetus. Those opposed to the availability of abortions are more concerned with "the right to life" than the "right to choose."

Largely as a result of the contemporary politics surrounding abortion, an ideology of sexual freedom and the right to control one's own body has found a home in contemporary sexual debates, especially those within contemporary feminism. Accordingly, in Chapter 4 I demonstrate the ways in which COYOTE and its affiliates adopted this language to legitimate their position on prostitution. I also detail how prostitution, as a form of sex for sale, presents a difficult issue for feminists concerned with addressing the issue of violence against women as well as the right to privacy and self-determination (Leidholdt and Raymond 1990; Overall 1992; Seidman 1992).

PORNOGRAPHY AS A SOCIAL PROBLEM

Although pornography has existed for centuries in the United States, in the last two decades it has been politicized more than ever. As a result of debates between antipornography groups and their critics, pornography has been institutionalized as a social problem and placed at the center of contemporary sexual politics. More specifically, during the last two decades pornography has emerged as a highly visible and politically volatile issue that sits at the intersection of public discussions on victimless crimes, violence against women, and constitutional rights to privacy and the freedom of expression. As a result, it is the antipornography campaigns of the 1970s and 1980s, complete with vehement supporters and detractors, which provided the national forum for the prostitutes' rights movement to press claims about sex for sale generally. This forum was supported by a preoccupation with public debates and legal redress.

Pornography as a Legal Issue

It is important to distinguish between pornography as a popular term and obscenity as a legal concept. Pornography comes from the Greek work *porneia,* which simply means prostitution or writings of prostitutes (Hyde 1982; Young 1964). In general usage, pornography refers to literature, art, film, speech, and so on, that is or is presumed to be sexually arousing in nature. Pornography may be soft-core, that is, suggestive, or hard-core, which usually means that there is explicit depiction of sexual activity in the material.

Strictly speaking, pornography has never been illegal. However, from a legal standpoint, pornography is often equated with obscenity, which is illegal. The word *obscene* suggests that which is foul, disgusting, or lewd. *Obscene* or *obscenity* is used as a legal term for that which is offensive to the authorities and/or communities (Wilson 1973). The issue of obscenity has received legal redress since the Supreme Court decided that obscenity was not protected by the First Amendment.

There is a long history of judicial efforts to delineate criteria of obscenity, which would identify material not protected under the free speech and free press guarantees of the Constitution. Numerous landmark decisions have been handed down by the Supreme Court to set limits on the expression of sexual behavior in the publicly available media. In *United States v. Roth* (1957), the court ruled that obscenity is "material which deals with sex in a manner appealing to prurient interest" (quoted in Hyde 1982, p. 554). Also in 1957, the Supreme Court ruled that materials are pornographic if they not only appeal to essentially "prurient interests," but oppose "contemporary community standards" and are "utterly without redeeming social value" (quoted in Jones et al. 1988, p. 208). As a result of decisions such as these, the identification of community standards is a significant social and legal dilemma.

In 1973, the year COYOTE emerged, the Supreme Court again tried to define obscenity in *Miller v. California.* Chief Justice Burger and the four concurring justices proposed determining whether or not something is pornographic by considering the following frequently cited criteria:

> (a) whether the average person, applying contemporary community standards, would find that the work, taken as a whole, appeals to the prurient interests, (b) whether the work depicts or describes, in a patently offensive way, sexual conduct specifically defined by the applicable state law, and (c) whether the work, taken as a whole, lacks serious literary, artistic, political, or scientific value. (quoted in Hyde 1982, p. 555)

The result of this decision was to define hard-core pornography as obscene and to require from state statutes precise descriptions of that which is to be illegal. Of course, such descriptions rely upon local community standards, and thus remain open to debate and change. Whatever their focus, however, obscenity laws deny the right of free expression to those who transgress official standards of propriety and, by extension, harm the community.

Current Debates over Pornography

English, Hollibaugh, and Rubin have correctly observed that, regardless of a history of legal gerrymandering, pornography "pushes people's buttons. They polarise and go to their corners very fast" (1981, p. 43). As advocates and activists on both sides run to their corners, the controversy has been over whether pornography should be outlawed in the interest of public morality or decriminalized as an expression of individual liberty.

These two positions are most often represented by conservatives and cultural feminists at one end of the continuum, and civil libertarians and sex-radical feminists at the other.[4] The libertarians and sex-radical feminists emphasize pleasure, while the conservatives and the cultural feminists emphasize danger, (Ferguson, Philipson, Diamond, Quinby, Vance, and Snitow 1984; Snitow et al. 1983; Vance 1982, 1984; Weeks 1985).

Conservatives and Cultural Feminists

People oppose the production, distribution, and consumption of pornography for different reasons, many of which parallel the reasons offered for the acceptance or abolition of prostitution. Historically, conservative analysts and constituencies have believed that pornography cheapens and demeans human sexuality through a "general degeneration of moral susceptibilities and a divorcement of sex from context" (Weeks 1985, p. 234). Moreover, they are concerned that pornography encourages the proliferation of sex-related crimes. For example, a nationally publicized 1986 attorney general's report documented testimony that hard-core pornography was used by a majority of child molesters, rapists, and incest offenders. The publication of such documents has served to cement pornography's historical connection to crime.

In addition to crime, conservative antipornography groups have connected pornography to a general moral decline. Groups such as the Citizens for Decency Through Law, Inc., have argued that pornography has become a dangerous part of American culture. Central to their crusade is the belief that pornography is morally wrong, inherently disgusting, and both a contributing factor to and a reflection of increasing moral decay. As such, the production and consumption of pornography must be suppressed through public education and legal remedies.

Long a concern of conservatives, pornography became a central preoccupation of contemporary feminism in the late 1970s and throughout the 1980s. Many feminists joined conservatives in their fight against pornography (Bell 1987; Bessmer 1982; Diamond 1980; Ferree and Hess 1985). In the process, cultural feminists have offered different analyses and justifications for the suppression of pornography. While traditional moralists are worried about pornography's connection to crime and moral decay, cultural feminists' ostensible concern has not been with the effect of explicit sex on the male viewer. Instead, they are primarily concerned with sexual images that are considered to evoke and legitimate violence against women through the perpetuation of a misogynist culture (Barry 1979; Brownmiller 1975; Diamond 1980; Dworkin 1981; Griffin 1982; Lederer 1980; MacKinnon 1982, 1983).

From a cultural-feminist point of view, pornography teaches men to view women as sex objects, justifies the use of women's bodies for men's pleasure, and contributes to the general victimization of women in society. From this perspective, the central contention is that pornography is intimately connected to violence against women. Cultural feminists argue that pornography harms women in specific and general ways. First, women used in the production of pornographic material are exploited.

At the same time, pornography creates and justifies hostility toward women in general, which contributes to the high rate of crimes and other abuses against women. As the often cited slogan of Morgan explains, "porn is the theory, rape is the practice" (1978, p. 169).

At the heart of the cultural-feminist antiporn project is an analysis that views pornography as "the undiluted essence of antifemale propaganda" (Brownmiller 1975, p. 443). In a chapter entitled "Pornography: The Ideology of Cultural Sadism," Barry explained:

> The most prevalent theme of pornography is of utter contempt for women. In movie after movie women are raped, ejaculated on, urinated on, anally penetrated, beaten, and, with the advent of snuff films, murdered in an orgy of sexual pleasure. Women are the objects of pornography, men its largest consumers, and sexual degradation its theme. . . . Racism and sexism blend with the other characteristics of pornography to provide entertainment based on sexual objectification, violence and contempt for women. It is the media of misogyny. (1979, p. 175)

The bottom line for cultural feminists is that pornography is the distillation of male power over women, and as such it is an institutionalized vehicle through which women's subordinate status is perpetuated.

This analysis justifies the fervor and moral passion that infuses the cultural-feminist antipornography campaigns, in which legal redress has figured prominently. For example, Catherine MacKinnon, Andrea Dworkin, and other feminists have pressed various municipalities to institute antipornography ordinances. Such ordinances would allow women to sue on a tort basis the manufacturers or sellers of pornography by claiming personal harm, and/or violation of individual civil rights. In effect, ordinances like this legitimate censorship under the banner of women's civil rights.

Along with legal redress, three major feminist antipornography organizations emerged in the 1970s with the avowed purpose of enlightening the public about the dangers associated with, if not caused by pornography. Women Against Violence in Pornography and Media (WAVPM) was established in the San Francisco Bay Area, Women Against Pornography (WAP) was established in New York City, and Women Against Violence Against Women (WAVAW) was established in Los Angeles. Supported by cultural-feminist suppositions, groups such as these declared an all-out war on pornography and continue to fight against the obstacles posed by opponents. In so doing, they have been greatly responsible for the widespread recognition of pornography as a social problem. In large part, they have done this by instigating and engaging in local and national

NO

public debates where they advocate a cultural-feminist analysis of pornography.

The feminist antipornography movement has galvanized many women and constituencies across the country. As Weeks observed, "in the United States by the early 1980s the feminist campaigns against pornography were perhaps the best organized and financed in the movement's history" (1985, p. 231). As a result, the media have embraced the cultural-feminist perspective on pornography as *the* feminist position on pornography (Ehrenreich, Hess, and Jacobs 1982; Snitow et al. 1983; Rubin 1984). Although this (arguably) remains the dominant feminist analysis of pornography and sex for sale in this country (Leidholdt and Raymond 1990), such an analysis of sex for sale has not gone uncontested.

Civil Libertarians and Sex Radicals

By the midseventies, pornography became *the* focus for feminist discussions of sexuality (Ehrenreich et al. 1982). As cultural-feminist arguments against pornography were being institutionalized, the issue of pornography seemed to be dividing the women's movement—there has been strong opposition to the cultural feminists' approach to pornography inside the women's movement. Along with civil libertarians, sex-radical feminists have suggested numerous critiques of the position expressed by conservatives and cultural-feminists.

The sexual assumptions of the antipornography crusade and cultural-feminist analyses of pornography have become a springboard for countervailing feminist politics. Civil libertarians and sex-radicals have emerged to stress the right to sexual variety and pleasure, while cautioning against the suppression of sexual dissidence (in this case, commercialized sex). Moreover, critics of the antipornography movement have taken it to task for its sensationalism, moralism, and biased emphasis on female victimization (Echols 1983; Ellis 1984; Elshtain 1982a, 1982b; English et al. 1981; Rubin 1984; Rubin and Califia 1981; Willis 1981, 1982, 1983).

Civil libertarians and sex-radical feminists have joined forces to claim that antipornography groups' method of protest could undermine the constitutional rights of free speech and freedom of expression, encourage the suppression of ideas and sexual expression, and possibly even lead to censorship. Willis succinctly stated the sex radicals' view on the repressive nature of the antipornography crusades:

> The basic purpose of obscenity laws is and always has been to reinforce cultural taboos on sexuality and suppress feminism, homosexuality and other forms of sexual dissidence. . . . [N]ot too

> long ago information about female sexuality, contraception, and abortion was assumed to be obscene. In a male supremacist society the only law that will not be used against women is no law at all. (1983, p. 466)

This position asserts that consenting adults should be allowed to engage in all forms of sexual behavior without being at the mercy of others', including feminists', understandings of what constitutes appropriate or moral behavior.

Civil libertarians and sex-radical feminists argue that the state has no business regulating morality in any realm, but especially in the sexual realm. The First Amendment guarantee of freedom of expression is consistently invoked to suggest that the allowance of sexual behavior does not—and should not—hinge on moral judgments of artistic merit or even redeeming value. To civil libertarians and sex-radical feminists, the conservative and cultural-feminist position on pornography represents an attack on sexual civil liberties and sexual freedom insofar as it directly and/or indirectly favors censoring commercialized sex.

In order to oppose antipornography campaigns, civil libertarians and sex-radical feminists often argue that the harm associated with pornography is absent or negligible, but certainly ambiguous. Sex radicals challenge the fundamental proposition that there is a *demonstrable* relationship between pornography and violence against women. They deny the cultural-feminists' assumptions about the connection between fantasy and reality by negating the purported empirical connection between violence against women and the "recreational" use of pornography.

By proposing a weak connection between "monkey see, monkey do," sex-radical feminists have argued that there is little or no *observable* empirical relationship between pornography and violence against women. Echols, for example, warns:

> While the elimination of violence [especially against women] is crucial, there is reason to be dismayed by the [feminist antiporn] movement's assumption, despite the dearth of solid, confirming evidence, that pornography is a causative factor. And, there is reason to be alarmed by its casual attitude toward establishing causality. For instance, Kathleen Barry has urged against getting "bogged down in academic research" and urged us to "rely more on our common sense, our own convictions." (1983, p. 448)

In agreement is Ellis, who argued that:

> The argument for a causal relationship between pornography and violence against women assumes a virtual seamless connection be-

> tween behavior, fantasy, and the unconscious, as if each were a replication of the other in a different mode. (1984, p. 122)

Finally, Willis notes that "if *Hustler* were to vanish from the shelves tomorrow, I doubt the rape or wife-beating statistics would go down" (1983, p. 463). In offering statements such as these, sex-radical feminists have relentlessly questioned the degree to which pornography is associated with harm against women.

Sex-radical feminists go one step further to suggest that there are qualitative distinctions in material that is categorized as pornography, and it is not appropriate to condemn all of it.[5] They argue that pornography can have some redeeming qualities. For example, they claim that some pornography acts as a safety valve and actually *decreases* sex crimes (McCormack 1978). In the same vein, feminists opposing the antipornography project have conceived of pornography as a freely chosen activity that actually benefits some women's lives. In one of the earliest public feminist critiques of the growing antipornography movement, Willis proclaimed the following in 1979:

> Over the years I've enjoyed various pieces of pornography . . . and so have most women I know. Fantasy, after all is more flexible than reality, and women have learned, as a matter of survival, to be adept at shaping male fantasies to their own purposes. If feminists define pornography per se as the enemy, the result will be to make a lot of women ashamed of their sexual feelings and afraid to be honest about them. And the last thing women need is more sexual shame, guilt, and hypocrisy—this time served up as feminism. (1983, p. 462)

In another publication, Willis goes further, suggesting that pornography contains elements of resistance to patriarchal structures:

> We must take into account that many women enjoy pornography, and that doing so is not only an accommodation to sexism, but also a form of resistance to a culture that would allow women no sexual pleasure at all. (1982, p. 17)

In this light, pornography is viewed as a tolerable, acceptable, and liberating.[6]

Regardless of how the pornography debates continue to unfold, they nonetheless render visible the way in which differential assessments of harm, consent, and constitutional rights are at the center of the contemporary discourse on sex. Where one falls in the contemporary debates on pornography is, no doubt, largely determined by assessments of the

NO

degree of harm associated with pornography and the scope of individuals' rights to expression and privacy. Not surprisingly, this point of contention is mirrored in contemporary debates over prostitution.

PROSTITUTION AS A SOCIAL PROBLEM

Contemporary discourse on prostitution as a social problem emanates from two general domains. First, debates about prostitution as a victimless crime are found in the legal arena, especially among legislators and law enforcement officials. Discussions of prostitution as a social problem are also located in moral reform discourse, especially that which emanates from both nineteenth-century and contemporary feminism. Combined, these contributors have established the ways in which prostitution has been conceived in this country. By extension, they have established the political backdrop for the contemporary prostitutes' rights movement.

Prostitution as a Victimless Crime

In most jurisdictions in the United States, prostitution is officially classified as a victimless crime. However, in the United States it is not, strictly speaking, a crime to be a prostitute; rather, it is a crime to engage in sex for sale. With the exception of a few rural counties in Nevada, prostitution is illegal in every jurisdiction in the United States. Although laws vary by state, there are generally two types of laws controlling prostitution: (1) laws prohibiting loitering with the intent to commit an act of prostitution, and (2) laws against offering and/or agreeing to an act of prostitution. The law also forbids activity related to prostitution, such as solicitation, pandering, pimping, procuring, renting premises for prostitution, loitering, vagrancy, and enticing minors into prostitution.

Prostitutes have been conceived as sexual criminals, victims of sexual crimes, and contaminated women by law enforcement officials, moral crusaders, and public health officials, respectively. Along with viewing prostitutes as victims of illicit sex, law enforcement agencies have historically viewed prostitution as condemnable because of its close connection to other crimes. Organized crime, larceny, robbery, assault, and narcotics are often cited as crimes associated with prostitution. A classic argument is that such crimes proliferate in the environment fostered by prostitution (D'Emilio and Freedman 1988; Hobson 1987). As Sheehy argues, "what follows prostitutes is crime" (1974, p. 115). In addition, neighborhood decay is perceived to be closely associated with prostitution (Hobson 1987).

Nonetheless, prostitution is one of the most common reference points for the discussion of the decriminalization of victimless crimes. Historical arguments for the decriminalization of prostitution have rested on the assertion that police efforts at curbing prostitution seem to be expensive, unsuccessful, and open to corruption and dubious organizational practices. If prostitution were no longer defined as a crime, it is argued, all those involved—the prostitute, the customer, the police, and society at large—would benefit (Rosenbleet and Pariente 1973). In this view, prostitution is viewed as being a mutually agreed upon, much in demand, and relatively harmless activity.

Further, it has been suggested that much of the harm associated with prostitution, such as the victimization of women and the proliferation of crime, is a result of the *illegality* rather than the *practice* of prostitution (Alexander 1987a; Bell 1987; Caughey 1974). Some have questioned whether or not there is a victim in prostitution, and, if so, *who* the victim is. As Laws and Schwartz note, "while many persons appear to see prostitution as a transaction, some see the client as the exploiter and others, the prostitute" (1977, p. 125).

In light of prostitution's ambiguous relationship to individual and public harm, in the last few decades a number of groups in the United States have worked toward decriminalizing prostitution in this country: the National Organization for Women (NOW), the ACLU, sections of the American Bar Association, and the National Counsel on Crime and Delinquency. These organizations' efforts are anchored in a belief that prostitution represents a crime without a demonstrable victim, as well as a belief that sexual behavior between consenting adults should remain outside the purview of the law.[7]

Nineteenth-Century Feminist Discourse on Prostitution

Compatible with law enforcement's traditional stance toward prostitution, social reformers have been concerned with the prostitute as a victim of men's vices and illicit sex. Social and moral reformers have historically viewed prostitutes with disdain and pity while arguing that prostitutes are degraded, exploited, and abused by the business of prostitution and the pimps behind it. With this view, the complete eradication of prostitution is the only way to protect women from harm *and* to protect society from the prostitute (D'Emilio and Freedman 1988; Hobson 1987; Sheehy 1974). Like the conservatives in the pornography debates, moralists concerned with prostitution have defined sexual promiscuity as a sin and therefore prostitution as a contributing factor to the alleged moral decay of American society.

Over the last 125 years, prostitution has represented a difficult issue for feminists. The early social purity movements in the United States and England included campaigns to abolish prostitution. The purity crusades of the nineteenth century afforded feminists, who were allied with repressive moralists and antisuffragists, some control over sexual politics. This was accomplished by starting a public discourse on sex and mobilizing against male vice (D'Emilio and Freedman 1988; Ferree and Hess 1985; Walkowitz 1980, 1983).

By advocating the repeal of the Contagious Disease Acts of 1864, many nineteenth-century feminists produced an abstract image of prostitutes as victims of illicit sex and male vice. Male vice, at least in this case, was lust, which was seen as the source of women's slavery. This conception then became a primary justification for the control of prostitution by establishing a state apparatus of protectionist sexual politics (Ferree and Hess 1985; Snitow et al. 1983; Walkowitz 1980, 1983). At the heart of feminists' participation in the purity crusades were two beliefs. First, feminists believed that women were harmed by engaging in prostitution. Specifically, they were victims of "male pollution, as women who had been invaded by men's bodies, men's laws, and the 'steel penis,' the speculum [which was used in performing required gynecological exams]" (Walkowitz 1983, p. 422).

Second, they argued that the harm in prostitution was a direct result of male vice, in this case the demand for illicit sex. These feminists were adamant about ensuring women's rights to be protected from male abuse, which was epitomized by prostitution. They saw prostitution as a paradigm for the female condition, a symbol of women's powerlessness and sexual victimization (D'Emilio and Freedman 1988; Ferree and Hess 1985; Walkowitz 1983). One identifiable subtheme of this discourse was that females of all classes and backgrounds were vulnerable to male sexual violence, especially in the form of prostitution.

Walkowitz describes the image of prostitution produced by nineteenth-century feminists as "constrained around a limited vocabulary—constructed around the theme of victimization" (1983, p. 423). They focused on the coercive nature of prostitution, while discussions of its lucrative and/or voluntary aspects received far less publicity. As Snitow et al. observe:

> Blinkered by their own experiences as middle-class women, the social purity feminists were entirely unable to perceive the ways in which other women—their own working class sisters—could act as sexual agents rather than as victims, using sex to further their own purposes and pleasures. (1983, p. 419)

The attempts to protect young working-class women were based on a desire to control their sexuality by prohibiting them from engaging in commercial sex of any form. Thus, the social purity movement supported middle-class interests even as it recruited support from working-class constituencies.

Contemporary Feminist Discourse on Prostitution

As a highly visible form of commercialized sex, prostitution has been at the center of contemporary feminist debates on sexuality and violence against women. Like in the feminist debates on pornography, contemporary feminists have been caught between two opposing views (Leidholdt and Raymond 1990; Overall 1992). On the one hand, the objectification and commoditization of women's bodies is seen to be exemplified in prostitution. From this perspective, the abolishment of prostitution has been advocated. On the other hand, a central tenet in feminism has been the belief that women should be ensured the right to self-determination, especially with regard to their bodies and sexuality. In this light, the abolishment of prostitution is seen as repressive sexual politics. In large part, these positions parallel the positions on pornography described earlier in this chapter. That is, the tension surrounding discussions of prostitution largely flows out of and reflects the views on pornography insofar as both are viewed as forms of commercialized sex. Since this tension is detailed in Chapter 4, what follows is brief and is only presented to provide a political backdrop for COYOTE's crusade.

Themes from the moral reform tradition of the nineteenth century continue to loom large in contemporary feminist concerns with exploitive sexuality, especially pornography and prostitution (Coward 1983; D'Emilio and Freedman 1988; Walkowitz 1983). Contemporary feminist debates over the status of prostitution in this country and others remain anchored in discussions of harm and coercion (Overall 1992). However, unlike in previous debates over prostitution, the prostitute's right to engage in self-proclaimed consensual commercial sex has served as a critical point of contention among varying feminist views. While contemporary feminist views on prostitution advocate the decriminalization of prostitution, they nonetheless continue to differ in the degree to which prostitution is legitimated as a form of commercial sex and a form of work (Alexander 1987a; Overall 1992).

In the main, contemporary feminist discourse on prostitution produces an image of prostitution that is engulfed in beliefs about the harm of commercialized sex and assertions about the exploitation of women associated with prostitution. Consistent with their stance on pornography, cultural feminists have approached prostitution as a form of commercialized sex. From this perspective, prostitution represents the ultimate degradation of women in that their bodies become commercialized objects (Barry 1979; Daly 1978; Morgan 1982). Moreover, in this view prostitution is *intrinsically* exploitive and oppressive to women. As such, it is a source and a reflection of women's victimization in patriarchal societies.

Therefore, prostitution must be decriminalized as a necessary first step in abolishing it altogether and ultimately "saving" women from the life of prostitution. As Chapter 4 demonstrates, images of prostitution articulated by feminist activists almost a century earlier have been affirmed and bear a striking resemblance to the image of prostitutes produced by cultural feminists today. While prostitutes are supported as women, prostitution is given no legitimation as a practice or as a career.

In sharp contrast, from a radical-feminist point of view the prostitute-client relationship is universally applicable to the relations between women and men, especially the relationship between husbands and wives, in all sexist societies. The focus is on commonalities in the political, economic, and social status of women vis-à-vis men. Courtship and marriage fundamentally reflect a socially enforced contract of sexual property (Collins 1971; Laws 1979; Rubin 1975). The extended argument is that all women sell their sexual favors to men for a price. Compared to the nonprostitute woman, the prostitute, however, sells her sexual favors in a less exclusive manner and without pretense (Bryan 1966; Goode and Troiden 1974; Jaget 1980; Millet 1971, 1974; Strong 1970). As Strong argued in the now classic *Sisterhood Is Powerful: An Anthology of Writings from the Women's Liberation Movement*:

> There is not as much difference between the hooker and the non-hooker as one might expect. In many ways the condition and dynamics of the hustler in American society parallels (in an exaggerated way, of course) the condition of women in general in this society. . . . Open any so-called women's magazine and one finds countless articles saying basically the same thing. Get what you can from a man and then "be nice" to him—but first, make sure that he's willing to provide you with those eminently desirable status symbols, ranging from the fur coat, ring, or necklace, to a box of chocolate-covered cherries. From the time a girl is old enough to go to school, she begins her education in the basic principles of hustling. Now there certainly is some conflict here, because on the one hand she is taught, verbally, to value love, self-worth, pride, compassion, and humanness, while on the other hand she is receiving distinct messages from those around her (from her parents on down through her favorite television personalities) that the real important goals are economic ascendancy and the status acquisition, and that she, a female, can acquire all these things if she plays her hand right. So, in reality, all the hustler has done is to eliminate

> the flowery speeches and put things where they're really at. Without the games, she will trade what is regarded as a commodity anyway, for what she wants. . . . All the prostitute has done is eliminate the bullshit. (1970, pp. 289–90)

Analogies such as this call attention to the close ties between prostitution and general patterns of female socialization and existence in patriarchal societies.

The argument is that there is an institutionalized element of prostitution in all male-female relations in patriarchal societies. What distinguishes prostitute from nonprostitute women is the degree to which such an element is made explicit and openly acknowledged. In addition to being a comparatively honest woman, the prostitute is in the best position to get a fair and definite exchange for her labor. In short, the prostitute has much in common with the nonprostitute; the primary difference is one of honesty and forthrightness in the sexualized encounter.

Finally, over the last fifteen years a relatively new perspective on prostitution has emerged and found a home within feminist ranks. Civil libertarian and sex-radical feminists have begun to argue that the issue of forced prostitution and its associated harm is often used to obscure the issue of the right of women to control their own bodies (i.e., to choose to engage in prostitution). From this perspective, prostitution should be decriminalized since the illegality of prostitution serves to institutionalize the denial of women's sexual self-determination. In short, everyone has the right to set the terms of their own sexuality, including its commercialization.

Like pornography, there is no agreement on the merits of prostitution. Moral reformers have pressed an array of analyses of and proscriptions for prostitution in order to assist in the handling (i.e., controlling or liberating) of the prostitute. Claims about the types of harm associated with prostitution and the degree to which women are coerced into or consent to prostitute themselves constitute the core of historical and contemporary prostitution politics.

In 1973 the sociopolitical milieu was ripe for the emergence of COYOTE's crusade to demand prostitutes' right to engage in consensual commercialized sex. After all, the 1960s and the 1970s witnessed a social and legal liberalizing trend. However, in the late 1970s and throughout the 1980s, the New Right played heavily in contemporary sexual politics. The New Right represents the most powerful source of claims that, in effect, advocate a return to traditional values, especially those demanding sexual regulation. The New Right's efforts to increase state regulation on sexual matters has presented an obstacle for the contemporary prostitutes' rights movement.

SEXUAL POLITICS AND THE NEW RIGHT

Up until the last decade and a half, it seemed reasonable to assume that sexual politics would continue to move in a liberal direction. Specifically, it seemed reasonable to assume that the right to privacy would eventually be extended to homosexual actions, sexual preference would be increasingly protected by statute, laws restricting consensual sex would slowly be removed from the law books, and the constitutional right to abortion would be protected. However, the early 1980s may well have proven to be the peak of sex law reform and liberal sexual politics, at least for the foreseeable future.

Social movements inevitably seem to produce countermovements based on resistance to social and legal change. Organized opposition to the decriminalizing of victimless crimes, the goals of the gay and lesbian movement, and the goals of the feminist movement emerged in the late 1970s in the form of the so-called New Right. As Ferree and Hess have noted in regard to the New Right, "they seek a massive repeal of real and imagined trends of the past four decades" (1985, p. 133). Right-wing opposition to sex education, homosexuality, pornography, sex research, contraception, and abortion have figured prominently in sexual politics throughout the 1980s.[8]

The New Right's attempt to regulate sexuality represents a dramatic countermove in a gradual long-term negotiation of sexuality (D'Emilio and Freedman 1988; Ferree and Hess 1985; Weeks 1985; Viguerie 1980). As Weeks noted, "we have witnessed a faltering, and retreat, of 'sexual liberation,' a resurgence of a political movement in defence of traditional norms" (1985, p. 16). By launching a direct attack on sexual liberalism in the broadest sense, the New Right has been relatively successful in delaying full implementation of the liberal sex laws already enacted. At the same time, the New Right has successfully inhibited further changes in sex-related statutes.

With its unifying motif of "the family" as the source of social and moral security, the New Right has widespread appeal (Conover and Gray 1983; D'Emilio and Freedman 1988; Ferree and Hess 1985; Klatch 1987; Rubin 1984). It has found its largest support among a constituency of embattled Christians; particularly powerful is the conservative evangelical sector, especially under the leadership of Jerry Falwell and his Moral Majority. However, it has also made its presence felt through middle-class women and through organizations such as Citizens for Decency (Davis 1981; Eisenstein 1981; Pankhurst and Homeknecht 1983).[9]

The New Right's growing strength throughout the 1980s and into the 1990s affected contemporary sexual politics in a variety of ways, all of which culminate in increased sexual regulation. For example, by targeting the prochoice movement, the "right to life" movement undertook a series of legislative campaigns to whittle away the right to abortion, especially by cutting off public funding for abortions. At the same time, the New Right has made questionable whether the notion of victimless crimes will be persuasive in the future. Representatives of the New Right seem determined to use the law to enforce a particular morality, which is based on heterosexual monogamy. For example, largely through the efforts of the New Right, many antidiscrimination laws supporting gay and lesbian rights have been defeated, as have domestic partner laws. Although the New Right's agenda is much contested, in a wave of conservatism the decriminalization of prostitution and other such victimless crimes is made increasingly problematic insofar as it is conflated with moral approval of the activities being removed from the purview of the law.

By the early 1980s the New Right had gained a massive following, and by the middle of the 1980s it had significantly impeded the liberal tendencies that preceded its emergence. The New Right has channeled a reservoir of support for limited legal changes, increasing controls on sexual behavior and free speech, and policies praising the primacy of the so-called traditional heterosexual nuclear family. In essence, the New Right is claiming a greater interest in the ownership of discourse on sexuality, and by extension the social control of sexuality.

The future of contemporary sexual politics is certainly an open-ended question. However, if the New Right has its way, it is quite possible that the liberalization of sexual politics has been extended as far as it is likely to go for quite sometime—at least until the current "conservative backlash" is successfully contested. With increasingly conservative state legislatures, and an increasingly conservative Supreme Court, we may well see a halt to the extension of the right to privacy in sexual matters in particular and other matters in general.

SETTING THE STAGE FOR A NEW MOVEMENT

Throughout the last thirty years there has been a virtual explosion of discourse on sex and sex-related matters. This discourse has primarily emanated from a social movement to decriminalize victimless crimes, the gay and lesbian movement, the contemporary feminist movement, and the New Right. Combined, these movements put into question, and made publicly debatable, issues of constitutional rights, consent, and harm as they relate to a variety of sexual practices and life-styles.

These public discussions have been anchored in attributions of personal and public harm, assessment of the degree to which sexual activity is consensual, and the scope of constitutional rights. In turn, this discourse has forced a sustained questioning of the place and limits of constitutional rights and consent, especially in a structure that places women in a subordinate status. Regardless of which side of the issue various constituencies advocate, they all must grapple with dilemmas of individual autonomy, legal constraint, constitutional rights, and assessment of the harm associated with sex. Seemingly inherent tensions between these substantive concerns continue to characterize contemporary sexual politics. In response to these tensions, legal redress and confrontational politics constitute the core of constituencies' political activities.

Regardless of the future of the gay and lesbian movement, the women's movement, the debates over pornography and prostitution as social problems, and the New Right, their presence has served to fundamentally shape the discourse of contemporary sexual politics. Specifically, since the so-called sexual revolution of the late 1960s and up to the conservative era of the 1980s, there has been an "erotization of the environment" (Gagnon and Simon 1973, p. 291) and a corresponding contest over the liberalization of sexual politics and sex-related laws. As a result, "what was once clandestine is now unabashedly public" (Goode and Troiden 1974, p. 3).

The recent participation of articulate self-proclaimed sex workers in sexual debates has marked a new stage in the discussion and creation of sexual politics in general and prostitution in particular. However, as the subsequent chapters detail, *how* COYOTE and its affiliates went about undertaking the contemporary prostitutes' rights movement was intimately connected to, and thus cannot be separated from, the sociopolitical milieu outlined in this chapter. Indeed, it is this larger political environment that set the stage for the emergence of COYOTE, provided a forum for the prostitutes' rights movement, and ultimately offered challenges to their efforts.

NOTES

1. Certainly, at any given moment numerous sets of discourse are prevalent in the social world. Foucault succinctly noted that when examining discourse on sex, "we are dealing less with *a* discourse on sex than with a multiplicity of discourses produced by a series of mechanisms operating in different institutions" (1980, p. 33). The term *discourse* is used in this work to refer to sets of general themes in the language used to discuss a particular social phenomenon, in this case sexual politics and the law.

2. Cataloguing statutes that fall within the realm of victimless crimes would be a difficult project if one considers federal law, military law, state laws, municipal codes, and county ordinances. There is a huge number of jurisdictions in the

United States, and an even larger number of statutes is applicable in those jurisdictions. Moreover, like other laws, laws related to victimless crimes are changing all the time. Thus, any list would be inaccurate shortly after it was compiled. However, Rubin has noted that "the only adult sexual behavior that is legal in every state is the penis in the vagina in wedlock" (1984, p. 291).

3. There is no single entity that can be labeled "the women's movement." As Ferree and Hess have demonstrated, "the New Feminist Movement is a loosely linked collection of formal organizations, occupational caucuses, friendship circles, collectives, and interest groups" (1985, p. 48). The same can be said of the gay and lesbian movement (Adam 1989).

4. Since gross categorizations such as this inevitably lead to objections, it is appropriate that the following disclaimer be offered: As identifiable strains of thought, these categories are generally agreed upon by analysts of the pornography debates (Leidholdt and Raymond 1990; Overall 1992). By maintaining that there is a theoretical coherence to these "types" of positions, I in no way mean to suggest that they are monolithic.

5. At this point, digressing into a review of the seemingly endless debates about what constitutes erotica, soft porn and hard porn would not be a fruitful detour.

6. Cultural feminists have responded to the claim that some women may benefit from pornography by arguing that such women have merely internalized the patriarchal culture that informs them. Cultural feminists argue that a truly feminist sexuality is not grounded in that culture, and it is not aroused by pornographic images, only images of tenderness and mutuality.

7. Unlike legalization, decriminalization would remove prostitution from the criminal code entirely and thus eliminate a need for legal definitions and involvement.

8. Although less important for this discussion of sexual politics, the New Right is also opposed to such things as progressive tax action, government regulation, weakness in foreign policy, gun control, communism, unions, and busing to achieve racial integration (Viguerie 1980).

9. Of course, these groups of supporters are not mutually exclusive.

3

COYOTE's Participation in Legal Discourse: Defining the Law as the Source of Prostitutes' Victimization

INTRODUCTION

Given the political environment described in the previous chapter, it is not completely surprising that COYOTE emerged in the early 1970s. A variety of minority groups were "coming out" to speak on their own behalf for the first time in history (Kitsuse 1980). As Weeks described:

> Transvestites, transsexual, paedophiles, sado-masochists, fetishists, bisexuals, prostitutes and others—each group marked by specific sexual tastes, or aptitudes, subdivided and demarcated often into specific styles, morals and communities, each with specific histories of self expression—have all appeared on the world's stage to claim their space and "rights." (1985, p. 187)

Clearly, COYOTE and the prostitutes' rights movement is in line with this historical moment, as well as compatible with numerous other constituencies emerging to be publicly counted, treated as legitimate, and granted rights of citizenship.

Consequently, in this chapter I describe the emergence of COYOTE and its grass roots campaign of the midseventies. The focus is on how COYOTE representatives sought support for their cause from prostitutes and reform-minded liberals by undertaking efforts designed to engage local law enforcement and city officials over the status of victimless crimes including prostitution, in the city of San Francisco. More broadly speaking, COYOTE's early campaigns were firmly located in legal discourse, especially existing debates surrounding whether or not to decriminalize sexual conduct between consenting adults, in this case between the prostitute and her client. Accordingly, this chapter details how COYOTE's challenges to and debates with law enforcement agencies and government officials over the status of prostitution as a victimless crime paralleled other local and national trends and debates, as described in the previous chapter.

What follows is a presentation of COYOTE's participation in legal discourse by documenting its claims about the removal of prohibitions against prostitution, legal discrimination against prostitutes, discriminatory enforcement of prostitution statutes, and the unjustifiable expense of enforcing prostitution laws. This is accomplished by documenting the substance of its local campaigns, as well as the types of counterclaims that emerged in response to COYOTE's early efforts. After describing COYOTE as a grass roots organization, I document each of these campaigns in an effort to understand the foundation of the organization's larger crusade.

THE FORMATION OF COYOTE

Before turning to COYOTE's early campaigns, it is useful to provide an overview of the formation of COYOTE as a grass roots organization with Margo St. James at the helm. Therefore, first there is a brief description of COYOTE in terms of its origins, leadership, recruitment strategies, structure, and community services. As will become evident, most of the characteristics of COYOTE as a social movement organization reflect COYOTE's initial concerns with the laws prohibiting prostitution, and law enforcement's procedures for curtailing prostitution.

Origins

Although the overarching goal of COYOTE has been the decriminalization of prostitution, the organization was originally formed to instigate and sponsor protests designed to bring attention to the abuses of local prostitutes and to provide numerous community services to women and prostitutes. COYOTE emerged on Mother's Day in 1973 from an organization called WHO, which is an acronym for Whores, Housewives, and Others.[1] The Point Foundation at Glide Memorial Church provided St. James, a self-proclaimed ex-prostitute, with a five thousand dollar grant in order to organize San Francisco's first prostitutes' "union." Shortly thereafter, St. James was given one thousand dollars from the Playboy Foundation to support COYOTE's efforts.

St. James recruited fifty influential San Franciscans to form an informal advisory board, as well as local prostitutes to advocate reform. Less than a year after COYOTE's founding, a newspaper explained that "thanks to Miss St. James' celebrity status in San Francisco, COYOTE has a board, which includes judges and artists" (Farguharson 1974, n.p.). Interested parties, including students, clients of prostitutes, politicians, media personnel, activists, and representatives from other advocacy organizations were invited and encouraged to become members of COYOTE. In short, anybody could become an active or an honorary member of COYOTE by simply paying a small membership fee.

Leadership

St. James was the main recruiter and coalition builder for COYOTE from its inception until 1986. As the founding "chairmadam" of COYOTE, St. James has been described as "a charming, indefatigable and articulate ex-hooker" (Farguharson 1974, n.p.), "a natural celebrity" (Milner and Hawkins 1976, n.p.), and "articulate, brash, enterprising and determined" (Rubin 1986, n.p.). In one of the first published historical accounts of COYOTE, Hobson explained that St. James's

> wholesome, athletic look and zany style made her an instant media personality. Newspapers and broadcast talk shows sought out St. James for interviews, and even the established old guard, the San Francisco Barristers Club, invited her to speak about prostitution reform. (1987, p. 216)

Similarly, in "The Oldest Profession Organizes at Last," *Ms. Magazine* reported that COYOTE's early support

> is entirely because of St. James' drawing power, which seems to be based on her genuine liking for people, coupled with a shrewd exploitation of herself. Her conversation is humorously profane, full of bawdy puns and frank revelations about her sexual tastes, all intermingled with serious rhetoric about her mission to change the laws and image of prostitution. (Braudy and Thom 1973, p. 17)

As the main spokesperson for COYOTE, St. James was soon widely known by the local legal community, including judges, district attorneys, detectives, police, pimps, prostitutes, lawyers, and bail bondsmen (Thomas 1978). As one reporter surmised, "St. James is practically a household word in the Bay area" (Rubin 1986, n.p.). As a result of her involvement in the prostitutes' rights movement, St. James immediately became something of a media celebrity at the local level, and eventually at the national level. With regard to the former, the first year of COY-

OTE's existence, the *Seattle Post-Intelligencer* reported that "Margo is 'in' socially this year. Well-to-do liberals invite her to things and seek her company" (Clever 1973, p. A18). By the early 1980s, St. James's celebrity status had extended to the national level (Caidin 1983; Cherrington 1980; Donahue 1980). Indeed, one talk show host introduced her as "the best known prostitute in the world" (Cherrington 1980).

Recruitment

Despite St. James's personality and consistent media attention as a resource, the recruitment of working prostitutes proved to be difficult. At least in part, this difficulty was born of prostitutes' fear of being identified publicly, as well as their fear of reprisal from law enforcement. As *The Daily Californian* reported, "since prostitution is illegal, prostitutes could hardly be expected to reveal themselves as such to voice their complaints against the system" (Brown 1974, p. 9). In a personal interview, St. James explained that the most significant difference between organizing prostitutes in Europe, where prostitution is legal, versus the United States, where it is illegal, has to do with fear of legal reprisal. She said: "It's easy to have working prostitutes involved there [in Europe] 'cause it's not an illegal job. And they don't have to wonder which one of the people at the meeting is the snitch" (personal interview, June 20, 1989).

In a strict legal sense, it is illegal for prostitutes to organize. By associating with each other, prostitutes can be seen as "conspiring" and/or "pimping," and are vulnerable to arrest and prosecution. A number of prostitutes associated with COYOTE have described the fear that goes along with joining the organization. For example, Carol Leigh, a prostitute, an outspoken prostitutes' rights activist, and a member of COYOTE explained:

> Our potential astounds me, but the fact that prostitution is illegal paralyzes me. Am I allowed to organize with other prostitutes? I don't think I'm allowed to talk to another prostitute. That might be conspiracy. (Delacoste and Alexander 1987, p. 157)

Despite the obvious threats posed by joining the organization, self-proclaimed working prostitutes emerged to claim affiliation with COYOTE. For example, a working prostitute in Brighton, Massachusetts, wrote the following in a letter sent to COYOTE's main office:

> I have been working in the streets of Boston for 1/2 year as a streetwalker. Several working girls I know are interested in orga-

> nizing a similar group as COYOTE. We are trying to pull together an organization from scratch. I intend to serve as an advisor until the organization can function without my help. We would appreciate, greatly, any information, advice, and moral (or immoral) support you can give. I am enclosing $6 for a general membership and $2 for a COYOTE button. (Schlesinger Library Holdings)

In a more public manner, Lucy, then a Chicago-based prostitute and COYOTE representative, explained in an interview with the *Chicago Sun Times*:

> Many hookers are afraid to come out, and many of the pimps don't want them to join. But they will join even though now it can be very dangerous for some of these women to come out in public. It's a slow process but it's coming. We have to fight this down of society that labels you a criminal. . . . If we joined together, we could fight that. (Kellog 1974, p. 24)

COYOTE leaders were hopeful that working prostitutes would organize and come out publicly to advocate on their own behalf, despite a recognition of the possible hazards imposed by such attempts.

Within the first year of its formation, COYOTE *claimed* a membership of over one thousand, 10 percent of whom were active prostitutes (Ritter 1973). In 1973 St. James *reported* making contact with 15–20 percent of San Francisco's prostitutes, while enlisting about 10 percent of San Francisco's five thousand prostitutes (Bryan 1973a, 1973b). Despite what may seem to be a small percentage of local prostitutes recruited to participate in COYOTE's efforts, St. James explained that "enrollments are phenomenal because they are a paranoid group" (Bryan 1973b, p. 2).

It is very difficult, if not impossible, to accurately assess how many members COYOTE and its affiliates have had at different points throughout their twenty-year effort. Clearly, a number of *self*-identified prostitutes have publicly claimed affiliation with COYOTE (as evidenced throughout this book). However, exactly how many prostitutes have been members is open to debate. At the same time, exactly how many nonprostitutes have been/are members of COYOTE (and its affiliates) is difficult to determine. COYOTE headquarters in San Francisco has sporadically kept membership lists in rather professional-looking ledgers. A review of these ledgers reveals literally thousands of names and addresses. Unfortunately, however, the ledgers do not document the nature of these individuals' involvement in the organization(s). The analytic importance of this "invisible constituency" is addressed in Chapter 6.

Structure

Consistent with its "fluid" membership, COYOTE has no formal organizational structure—it can best be characterized as amorphous. St. James explained: "COYOTE was never actually any kind of corporate organization. It was the name for a concept I used to try to raise consciousness about prostitution and the need for decriminalization" (Rutter 1980, p. 15). However, over the years volunteers have been responsible for running the organization, which includes providing direct social services, taking legal action, and promoting educational campaigns. Individuals associated with COYOTE have done research on prostitution and formed an important part of COYOTE's initial information network. In addition, a number of lawyers and lawyers' groups, most notably the ACLU and Barristers' Clubs, have contributed time and counsel to the organization.

Compatible with its structure, COYOTE has "no paid staff and nobody officially designated to actually do anything" (Thomas 1978, p. 8). Active members of the organization serve a number of different functions, from data gathering to providing services to coalition building. COYOTE's organizational duties are very loosely defined. As Thomas described:

> In COYOTE everybody who had any connection with it was a practitioner, and there are no defined roles for practitioners—everybody did his or her "own thing." . . . A more smoothly operating organization might have brought about just as many changes, but it seems that part of COYOTE's success has been its looseness; the amorphousness of the organization has allowed it to work in a variety of ways it could not have had it been more tightly, traditionally structured. (1978, p. 8)

COYOTE's lack of paid positions and informal division of labor have characterized the organization since its inception. As St. James explained, "hookers don't like organization. They want a looser thing" (personal interview, June 20, 1989). Indeed, especially in the early years, COYOTE was referred to as a "loose women's organization." In this case, the word *loose* is a double entendre; it simultaneously refers to sexual promiscuity and organizational form.

Community Services and Early Campaigns

As a grass roots organization, COYOTE provided numerous services for prostitutes, most of which were designed to assist prostitutes in their dealings with the police and the courts. For example, COYOTE provided a hotline for prostitutes called SLIP (Survival Line for Independent Prostitutes), immediate legal assistance for prostitutes who had been arrested, suitable clothing for prostitutes making court appearances, around-the-clock legal advice and aid to arrested prostitutes, and in-jail classes designed to teach prostitutes survival skills (e.g., "How to Take Care of Yourself" and "How to Get In and Stay Out").

In addition to providing legal services to prostitutes, COYOTE undertook a number of public awareness campaigns in the early and midseventies. These campaigns implicated legal statutes surrounding prostitution and law enforcement practices as the problem with prostitution. Specifically, COYOTE's early campaigns centered around protesting: (1) the prohibition of prostitution; (2) rampant legal discrimination against prostitutes, especially police harassment and entrapment; (3) discriminatory enforcement of prostitution laws, especially along gender and race lines; and (4) the unjustifiable expenditure of tax revenue to control (i.e., arrest and prosecute) women arrested on prostitution-related charges. Combined, these campaigns located COYOTE's early activities firmly in local legal discourse as they pointed to the laws prohibiting prostitution and agents of law enforcement as the source of prostitutes' victimization.

PROMOTING DECRIMINALIZATION

The year of COYOTE's inception, St. James announced that "changing the law is, of course, the most important job" (Bryan 1973a, p. 1). Since then, COYOTE's overarching goal has been the decriminalization of prostitution. Unlike the legalization of prostitution, the decriminalization of prostitution would remove all statutes prohibiting solicitation, pimping, pandering, and prostitution. In *Sex Work: Writings By Women in the Sex Industry* (Delacoste and Alexander 1987), Alexander advocated the decriminalization of prostitution as a way of legitimating rather than abolishing prostitution:

> Ideally, decriminalizing would mean the repeal of all existing criminal codes regarding voluntary prostitution, per se, between consenting adults, including mutually voluntary relationships between prostitutes and agents or managers (pimp/prostitute relationships) and non-coercive pandering (serving as a go-between). (p. 209)

In effect, COYOTE representatives argued that if prostitution were decriminalized, as opposed to legalized, it would fall outside the purview of the law and prostitutes could lead *less* victimized lives.

From COYOTE's perspective, the illegality of prostitution is at the root of prostitutes' victimization. Specifically, the victimization of prostitutes stems directly from laws prohibiting sex for sale, which ensures that prostitutes remain open to abuse and have no legal recourse to take action against perpetrators of abuse. St. James pressed this position in an article entitled "Prostitutes as Political Prisoners," which appeared in a local newspaper:

> The illegality of the profession heaps abuse on the women that isn't inherent in the business itself. Men consider them to be legitimate victims, and the women suffer all kinds of brutalities and indignities at the hands of the customers and the cops. (1973, p. 9)

Early in COYOTE's crusade, claims such as this were most often pressed at the local level through the distribution of *COYOTE Howls*, as well as through the use of local newspapers and a variety of public forums.

Eventually, however, COYOTE's cause evoked media attention at the national level. For example, St. James commented on the nationally syndicated talk show "No Bull":

> I think you have to let them work and protect them. Give them legal recourse for exploitation and abuse. . . . I think if you take away the prohibition, you [also] take away the violence and the exploitation. You empower the worker. (Cherrington 1980)

On "The Donahue Show," St. James embedded similar claims about prostitution in contemporary understandings of the condition of women in general:

> We want to legitimize the work and allow women to keep the money they earn and to end the abuse that prohibition ensures. . . . To stigmatize women sexually through the criminalization of prostitution affects every woman. It gives men the power to sexually intimidate them in the office, in public, and in the home. (Donahue 1980)

In addition to protesting the statutes prohibiting prostitution, COYOTE's early campaigns were directed at local law enforcement and government officials responsible for the enforcement of the laws. For example, in response to then San Francisco mayor Joseph Alioto's campaign to "clean up" prostitution in San Francisco, St. James asserted the following in an interview with a local newspaper reporter:

> The worst part of prostitution is the illegality. I've asked hundreds of women in the business what the worst moment of degradation

> was and they answered unanimously that the true moment of humiliation and degradation is when they are busted. . . . The real degradation is at the hands of the police and the courts who divide women into two categories—whore and madonna. (Bryan 1973b, p. 2)

From COYOTE's perspective, "exploitation comes with the cops and the courts; otherwise, both people are getting what they bargained for" (Brammer 1974, p. 2); namely, the transaction they have mutually consented to and desire.

Framed in this way, and consistent with claims emanating from the larger movement to decriminalize victimless crimes (see Chapter 2), COYOTE's early claims culminated in suggesting that prostitutes and their customers should be allowed to undertake transactions that they both agree to without interference from the law. Moreover, from this perspective, the decriminalization of prostitution is required in order to discourage the systematic abuse of prostitutes and to ensure that prostitutes have legal recourse when abusive or exploitive situations arise. In short, the argument maintains that decriminalization of prostitution allows for a *reduction* in the victimization of prostitutes.

PROTESTING POLICE HARASSMENT

COYOTE's early efforts singled out police brutality and harassment as common practices that must be endured by local prostitutes as a result of the illegality of prostitution. COYOTE's campaigns publicized the ways in which law enforcement officials illegally enforce the legal statute. With slogans such as "Hookers Unite, You Have Nothing to Lose But Cop Harassment," "No More Jive in '75," and "My Ass Is Mine," COYOTE's local crusade opposed police harassment of prostitutes. This opposition was based on claims that it is the prohibition of prostitution, combined with prostitutes' lack of legal status, that promotes tolerance for police harassment of prostitutes. By extension, it is harassment, rather than illicit sex, that ensures prostitution is problematic.

It is not surprising that police harassment was one of the most immediate concerns of COYOTE. Prior to the formation of COYOTE, the gay community in San Francisco had successfully organized to protest police harassment and the right to participate in private, consensual sex. As St. James explained, "it's well past time for whores to organize. The homosexuals organized and now the cops are afraid to harass them anymore" (Bryan 1973b, p. 2). A local newspaper concurred, with the following report: "The homosexual community in San Francisco has gotten politically organized—just as the hookers are trying to do with their picket—and they put enough pressure on City Hall to stop entrapments" (Bryan 1973b, p. 2).

Riding on the heels of San Francisco's gay community's protests, COYOTE's antiharassment campaign included local protests and public announcements condemning local law enforcement for harassing prostitutes unnecessarily. For example, COYOTE members and supporters protested the use of downtown hotels by police to entrap prostitutes. As the press reported:

> The hookers looked like liberated housewives and the vice cops looked like the Mod Squad. The hookers and their friends were members of COYOTE. They had come to San Francisco's futuristic new Hyatt Regency Hotel to picket the place for being finky and providing vice-coppers with free rooms to entrap their sisters. . . . It was noon and the first day of a week long picketing campaign to bring public attention (and hopefully indignation) to bear on the increasingly frequent use of free rooms in fancy downtown hotels as "lurid set-ups" to which the vice-coppers bring suspected hookers. Once there, COYOTE says the cops entrap the girls into "soliciting" an act of prostitution. Most notorious of the hotels which give the cops their free entrapment rooms is the San Francisco Hilton which COYOTE picketed Oct. 23. Also picketed was the Bellevue Hotel on Oct. 24 and the Stanford Court on Oct. 25. So, COYOTE's campaign got underway in a light drizzle with at least 20 pickets, half a dozen vice cops and six or eight newspaper and television reporters on hand. The signs said: "OFF THE PUSSY PATROL," "MY ASS IS MY OWN," "STOP ENTRAPMENT," "DOES IT HAVE TO BE BAD TO BE GOOD?" and a lot more (Bryan 1973a, p. 1).

Included in COYOTE's antiharassment campaign was a proposal for local law enforcement officials to treat prostitution as a victimless crime by issuing citations for prostitution rather than arresting prostitutes. COYOTE and its supporters tried to persuade the courts to treat solicitation as a form of disorderly conduct, with both customers and prostitutes fined like traffic violators. As St. James explained in an interview with a local paper:

> The citation campaign is crucial not to the campaign for decriminalization, but crucial to ending the counter-productiveness of the present arrest, incarceration program . . . also crucial to the City's revenue crisis. They know they spend at least $5 or $5 million

> arresting prostitutes. The citation thing would end a lot of our problems. (Bryan 1974, p. 2)

Moreover, COYOTE and its supporters proposed that the money received by the authorities go into "a scholarship fund for women in the life who are interested in achieving alternative means of survival" (Farguharson 1974, n.p.).

COYOTE's proposal to issue citations for prostitution rather than arresting prostitutes prompted attention from the press, primarily as the source of heated debate in at least three City Board of Supervisors meetings. Following the headline, "Will Supervisors Screw Whores?" a local paper reported that: "COYOTE participated prominently in the October 24th Board of Supervisors hearing on the question of issuing citations against those accused in 'victimless crimes' rather than hauling them down to jail for booking" (Bryan 1974). In each meeting, expert legal and medical testimony was offered in support of the proposal in general, and COYOTE's claims in particular.

COYOTE's proposal received support from a number of government officials, including then city supervisor John Molinari. As a local newspaper reported:

> Will certain members of the San Francisco Board of Supervisors end up screwing the town's whores as they play trade-off games of political accommodation aimed at winning over the most prudish and conservative of their colleagues so that we might finally embark on some kind of practical method of handling "victimless crime?" The Supervisors are finally getting hip to the fact that arresting and jailing people for victimless crimes (which are more violations of antiquated Christian morality than civil law) is not only grossly unfair and traumatic for the so-called "criminals," but damned expensive. It was, in fact, this latter consideration that got Finance Committee Member John L. Molinari into the act. (Bryan 1974, p. 1)

Packaged in this manner, the proposal was supported as a mechanism for implementing a revenue-saving and revenue-generating citation.

COYOTE's proposal to issue prostitutes citations rather than arrests was ultimately denied. However, it nonetheless generated media attention and local political controversy, which served to increase the visibility and viability of COYOTE's crusade by providing COYOTE representatives with a forum for the delivery of claims about the misuse of city funds and the welfare of local prostitutes.

OPPOSING SELECTIVE LAW ENFORCEMENT

Building on the claim that laws prohibiting prostitution and their enforcement are inherently problematic, COYOTE sought to expose the inequity of law enforcement procedures surrounding prostitution. As St. James adamantly noted in an interview with *Playgirl Magazine*, "the enforcement of prostitution is totally discriminatory" (Caruana 1974, p. 82).

COYOTE's early campaign brought attention to the unequal enforcement of the law on at least two counts. First, although solicitation is a crime for both the prostitute and the customer, typically only prostitutes, in most cases women, are arrested. In addition to systematic discrimination against women, COYOTE's campaign focused on the prevalence of racial discrimination in law enforcement's response to prostitution. A 1974 COYOTE newsletter explained on the front page: "COYOTE is dedicated to exposing sexism and racism within the Criminal Justice System and the furtherance of decriminalizing crimeless-crime" (*COYOTE Howls* 1974, p. 1). This general stance ensured that many assertions about gender and racial discrimination against prostitutes emanated from the prostitutes' rights movement early in its efforts.

Gender Discrimination

With slogans such as "The Trick Is Not Getting Caught," COYOTE pressed a series of claims directed at law enforcement officials' failure to arrest men involved in solicitation. As St. James explained in an interview with an Idaho newspaper, "there are a hell of a lot more customers than hookers, and the customers never get busted" (Brammer 1974, p. 2).

Claims such as these received a hearing from the national press. For example, in an interview with *Rolling Stone Magazine* St. James argued: "The enforcement of prostitution laws differs in every state depending upon the climate of the community, but they are all discriminatory in that they make women the scapegoat" (quoted in Krassner 1974, n.p.). Similarly, the *Washington Post* reported on St. James's approach and effectiveness:

> Margo meets her interviewers with xeroxed copies of papers by psychiatrists, sociologists and lawyers, all tending to demonstrate the laws on the subject are indefensibly biased in favor of the hooker's customer who never gets arrested and against the hooker who often does. (von Hoffman 1974, n.p.)

While the press was disseminating COYOTE's claims, a few local authorities were responding to and supporting COYOTE's efforts. For example, one San Francisco judge dismissed prostitution charges against thirty-seven women whose male customers were not arrested. She charged the police with an "intentional purposeful, selective enforcement policy" (Mydans 1976, n.p.). COYOTE was also central in convincing three female judges to participate in the women's political caucus and peer counseling to prostitutes.

Racial Discrimination

In addition to gender discrimination, COYOTE focused on the prevalence of racial discrimination in law enforcement's procedure for controlling prostitution. Combining claims of racism and sexism, St. James exclaimed to the press, "it's [the criminal justice system] racist and it's sexist and the only people who get arrested for prostitution are poor white women and blacks" (Bryan 1974, p. 8). With regard to racial discrimination in particular, St. James reported to the local press:

> Half of the women in the county jail are there on sex charges—political prisoners, arbitrarily chosen by society to pay its dues for sexual guilt. Most of them are black, another aspect of discrimination—minority women being forced to work on the street due to the fact that the hotels and massage parlors are owned by white folks who won't hire them or let them hang out. (Ritter 1973, p. 5)

Similarly, in an article entitled "A New Kind of Union to Help Woman-on-the-Street," Janine Bertram, a Seattle COYOTE representative, asserted:

> An organization like this [COYOTE] is necessary because of the discriminatory practices against prostitutes, the hassles on the street, the arrests for loitering and the entrapment by vice-squad men. Now, it's poor, often minority, women working the street who always get arrested, those who are unprotected. They get someone appointed by the court to represent them, don't have any bail and sit in jail from the weekend until the next Thursday when they go to court. For instance, in February, 25 black women were arrested for loitering. (Paynter 1975, n.p.)

Local press attended to COYOTE's campaign by reporting on, and thus disseminating, COYOTE's plea for legal reform. For example, a local magazine reported: "COYOTE is against the racism that exists with poor women of racial minorities making up the majority of those arrested while the white and higher paid call girls ply their trade in hotels and homes without arrest" (*San Francisco Magazine* 1973, p. 23). Through reports such as this, COYOTE's complaints were made public at the local level, and occasionally on the national level.

To further oppose the selective enforcement of prostitution laws, COYOTE instigated and/or sponsored at least twenty-six lawsuits on behalf of prostitutes. For example, with the support of the ACLU and the local Citizens Council for Criminal Justice, COYOTE filed numerous class action suits challenging the constitutionality of a California statute directed against anyone who solicits or engages in any act of solicitation. Suits were filed on the grounds that:

> It is an invasion of privacy, overly vague, and restricts freedom of expression, and that the state has no compelling interest in regulating sexual behavior between consenting adults, and therefore, that its selective enforcement violates the right to equal protection. (Anderson 1975, p. 41)

Through the public filing of these suits, COYOTE found yet another vehicle through which to disseminate pleas for legal reform. Clearly, these types of claims were firmly located in a larger discourse about the right to privacy and freedom of expression, which was being disseminated by the gay and lesbian community as well as the women's movement.

Along with filing lawsuits, COYOTE was successful in lifting a mandatory three-day venereal disease quarantine imposed by the San Francisco Police Department. In part, this was accomplished by pressing the claim that "the incidence of VD is at least as high among people 20 to 24 years old as among whores" (Anderson 1975, p. 41). Moreover, COYOTE made evident that "only women are arrested and forced to have regular checks for VD" (Metzger 1975, p. 8). Largely as a result of COYOTE's efforts, a San Francisco judge issued a temporary injunction ordering police to stop forcing suspected prostitutes to take penicillin shots and spend three days in jail until venereal disease test results came back. This temporary injunction was issued with an acknowledgment of the way in which such procedures constitute selective legal intervention.

CLAIMING TAX REVENUE IS WASTED

Building on the assertion that the enforcement of laws prohibiting prostitution is inherently problematic, COYOTE's campaign asserted that the enforcement of prostitution laws is simply a waste of taxpayers' money. Directed toward the San Francisco community in general, and law enforcement personnel in particular, COYOTE's protests suggested that it is a waste of taxpayers' money to enforce laws that create and perpetuate rather than eliminate the victimization of prostitutes. St. James suggested that "the real victim of victimless crime [such as prostitution] is the taxpayer" (Terzian 1974, p. 3).

Consistent with a the larger movement to decriminalize victimless crimes, from COYOTE's perspective it is a waste of law enforcement's time and resources to arrest prostitutes when there is no complainant. At a hotel protest, St. James claimed that "the police have their hands full dealing with real crime and they should not be distracted into pursuits concerning what consenting adults do" (Craib 1973, p. 2). Carol Silver, then legal counsel to the San Francisco Sheriff's Department and a proponent of COYOTE's efforts, concurred in an editorial in *COYOTE Howls*: "Society has a stake in decriminalizing prostitution so that resources presently allocated to catching ladies of the evening can be used instead for stopping crimes we're all really afraid of" (Silver 1974, p. 2). Relying upon a conception of prostitution as a crime without victims, COYOTE's protests and public pronouncements brought attention to the expense of enforcing prostitution laws. For example, St. James asserted to the local press:

> Thousands and thousands of tax dollars are being squandered each week by the vice squad. . . . While this city continues to be plagued by crimes against life and property, these overpaid officers are wasting their time and harassing people on non-victim charges. (Bryan 1973b, p. 2)

In an article entitled "COYOTE: Society's Underdogs Begin Biting Back," which was published in the local magazine *Pacific Sun*, St. James elaborated upon previous claims:

> The SFPD annual budget is 53 million, half of which is spent on victimless crimes. According to the 1971 report of the SF Crime Commission, taxpayers are paying $175 per bust for prostitution. Excessive labeling, for something which is essentially a service, not a crime, creates the criminal. It makes ROBs (rip-off-bitches) out of women, SOBs out of cops, and suckers out of taxpayers. (Ritter 1973, p. 4)

Finally, in an article in *COYOTE Howls* entitled "The Real Victim," an attorney volunteering her time and skill to COYOTE's campaigns claimed:

> The real victim in victimless crimes is you the tax payer. . . . Prostitution laws, like other laws directed at non-victim crime, originate in America's attempt to mandate a uniform code of morality, despite increased acceptance of alternative lifestyles. While police efficiency is such that a person who commits a crime against the person or property of a protesting victim has an 87% chance of never being arrested, police continue allocating resources to non-victim crime to such an extent that non-victim crime accounts for 50% of the arrests made. This is an expensive habit. For prostitution alone, the conservative estimate of $600,000 in direct costs per year nets approximately 654 arrests [in San Francisco]. We pay a huge price to attempt to enforce a given code of morality. (Terzian 1974, p. 3)

Assertions such as these suggest that prostitution is not only a crime without victims, but that it also represents a source of governmental waste.

While disseminating claims about the unjustifiable use of taxpayers' money to control prostitution, COYOTE also took direct legal action against the city's expenditure of funds to control prostitution: COYOTE instigated and supported two taxpayers' suits in San Francisco and Alameda Counties to decriminalize prostitution on the basis that it is a misuse of taxpayers' money (Ashley 1974, n.p.). Both of these suits facilitated the presentation of COYOTE's perspective to the local community and provided yet another avenue through which COYOTE's pleas were made public.

THE EMERGENCE OF LOCAL COUNTERCLAIMS

Within the first year of its existence, COYOTE had gained enough media attention and local support to force law enforcement and city officials to respond to their campaigns. As the *Seattle Post-Intelligencer* reported, "she's giving the San Francisco Police Department fits" (Clever 1973, p. A18). In response to COYOTE's assertions, city officials, especially law enforcement officials, offered counterclaims to dismiss COYOTE's pleas for reform. These counterclaims dismissed COYOTE's crusade by relying upon historically developed images of prostitution as a social problem associated with other violent and property crimes, the degeneration of neighborhoods, and the victimization of women. Each of these types of counterclaims is presented below in order to demonstrate that COYOTE's early efforts evoked a response, and to show the basis upon which COYOTE's efforts were contested.

Prostitution and Its Association with Other Crime(s)

Central to the assertions made in response to COYOTE's grass roots efforts was the suggestion that the use of taxpayers' money to control prostitution is well spent for a number of reasons. In the first place, law enforcement agents and government officials responded to COYOTE's claims by arguing that vice crimes such as prostitution represent the seeds of larger crime. For example, a San Francisco deputy district attorney publicly argued, "Vice-squad officers look at it the way I do. That there is something sort of subterranean [about vice crimes] which if left to grow and fester would overwhelm certain parts of the city" (Butler 1974, p. 6). Counterclaims such as these evoked and relied upon the historically developed image of prostitution as a precursor to and source of support for more serious crimes. Thus, so the argument goes, the control of prostitution is necessary for larger crime control efforts.

Neighborhood Decay

Continuing with the theme of public harm associated with prostitution, law enforcement agents and city officials also refuted COYOTE's claims by targeting prostitution as a source of neighborhood decay. For example, then San Francisco sheriff Dick Hongisto publicly acknowledged the selective enforcement of prostitution laws. He justified the discriminatory arrest of streetwalkers by pointing out the effects of their visibility:

> There are business interests in town that are very powerful. They believe that the only way to keep the city "clean" is to prosecute these things [prostitution]. They're not against prostitution per se, but street prostitution, the visible things that symbolize a "dirty city." (Butler 1974, p. 6)

From this perspective, prostitution constitutes a direct and indirect pollutant to the city. Thus, from the standpoint of law enforcement's counterclaims, prostitution—especially visible prostitution—requires containment in order to promote and maintain established community standards.

Illicit Sex and the Victimization of Women

City officials and law enforcement personnel also refuted COYOTE's demands for legal reform by denying the "victimlessness" of prostitution. Specifically, city official and law enforcement personnel promoted prostitutes' status as victims of illicit sex and the larger context within which commercialized sex occurs. In an interview with the local press, the inspector for the San Francisco vice squad offered a response to COYOTE's campaign against law enforcement:

> There's no such thing as a victimless crime. The prostitute is the victim in these crimes. She is usually the victim of a brutal pimp. I don't know any girl without a pimp—it's some kind of psychological necessity. (Bryan 1973b, p. 2)

From this point of view, the victimization of prostitutes by pimps justifies the enforcement of prostitution laws.

In direct response to COYOTE's campaigns, on rare occasion, representatives of the San Francisco Police Department (SFPD) conceded that enforcement of prostitution laws is selective, at least in terms of gender. However, they were quick to add that the selective nature of law enforcement's response to prostitution is justified from a law enforcement perspective. As then deputy district attorney Joe Russoniello, who headed the vice prosecutions, argued in an article entitled "On the Trial of Vice: The Crusade Against Sin on the Streets of San Francisco," that, "the customer is not involved with the commercial exploitation of sex, at least not on an ongoing basis" (Butler 1974, p. 6). In this light, women are viewed as victims of commercialized sex, while men are viewed as merely sporadic participants. Moreover, through the enforcement of prostitution laws, women are being protected from themselves in general and commercialized sex in particular. Framed in this way, the high arrest rates for women (prostitutes) and the comparatively negligible arrest rates for men (customers) is justifiable.

The emergence of numerous counterclaims dismissing COYOTE's demands increased the visibility of COYOTE's crusade. That is, at least in part, opposition to COYOTE's claims served to fuel COYOTE's campaign by creating local controversy. As local controversy developed, so too did media attention. However, COYOTE did not rely solely on controversy as a source of media attention to publicize the plight of prostitutes. It also relied upon self-promotion in the form of campy events, which became a civic resource for the city of San Francisco.

ATTRACTING MEDIA ATTENTION

Since its inception COYOTE has sent out information, attracted the press, provided speakers, organized lawyers, supported prostitutes in trouble, and fought hypocrisy in government and the courts. In the 1970s this activity was given visibility: Beginning in 1974 and ending in 1978, COYOTE staged a number of media events designed to raise funds, draw attention to the organization, and legitimate its campaigns. Most visibly, COYOTE staged two media events each year to generate revenue and public attention: the Annual Hookers' Convention and the Annual Hookers' Ball.

With the slogan "74, Year of the Whore," the First Annual Hookers' Convention was held in June 1974. San Francisco's Glide Memorial Church was packed with prostitutes, plainclothes police officers, city officials, news reporters, and interested spectators. National TV networks and news magazines covered this event, where a "Trick of the Year" award was given to a prostitute, and a giant keyhole was awarded to the "Vice Cop of the Year." The Second Annual Hookers' Convention was held in June 1975. This event featured numerous panels of experts who discussed the decriminalization of prostitution and a variety of related issues. Over twelve hundred people attended, including activists, lawyers, celebrities, and prostitutes.

The First Annual Hookers' Ball was held in October 1974 at the San Francisco Longshoreman's Hall. At this event, the theme was "No More Hippo Critters" and the song of the evening was "Everybody Needs a Hooker Once in Awhile." If the purpose of the ball, which was attended by such VIPs as state legislator Willie Brown and the San Francisco sheriff, was to draw attention to prostitutes and their cause, it was successful. As one newspaper stated, "it was something between the 1906 earthquake and fire, and the opening of the opera" (cited in James, Withers, Haft, and Theiss 1977, p. 73). The *Chicago Tribune* reported, "for the press it was an orgy. They filmed, photographed, and interviewed anyone who was generous with her eyeshadow" (Keegan 1974, p. 1). More locally, the *San Francisco Chronicle* described the events as "wild masquerades that drew the kind of people who really knew how to party [and that became] legendary, even though they lasted only a few years" (Rubin 1986, n.p.).

From 1974 to 1978 each Annual Hookers' Ball drew larger crowds and generated more funds than the previous one.[2] The 1977 ball grossed over ninety-three thousand dollars. According to the Bay Area Seating Service, over 1,160 publications throughout the United States and around the world covered it. Since the last Annual Hookers' Ball in 1978, however, COYOTE has relied upon private donations, honoraria, and government grants for its financial survival.

In addition to the balls and conventions, COYOTE sporadically published a newsletter, *COYOTE Howls*, which was sold to members of COYOTE, women's centers, women's bookstores, university libraries, and other interested individuals and organizations throughout the country. Primarily through *COYOTE Howls* and a speakers bureau, COYOTE has publicized accounts of police brutality and of abuse by customers. In so doing, COYOTE has sought to make its demands heard in a variety of arenas, especially legislatures and the media.

COYOTE's speakers bureau has provided speakers to a wide range of audiences, including legislatures, high schools, libraries, universities, barrister's clubs, women's groups, religious organizations, television and radio talk shows, scholarly conferences, and other groups interested in learning about prostitution. COYOTE has occasionally received small honoraria for providing speakers at such events. In addition, this has been a primary recruitment strategy for COYOTE.

GAINING RECOGNITION AND SUPPORT

As a result of increased visibility, COYOTE leaders developed an audience for COYOTE's crusade. Only seven months after COYOTE's inception, a local paper reported "Margo St. James is overwhelmed with speaking engagements, particularly before groups of law and medical students. . . . Sheriff Dick Hongisto has attended COYOTE meetings" (Ritter 1973, p. 4). Within the first few years of COYOTE's crusade, its speakers bureau received more requests for guest speakers than it could respond to, much less actually attend. Among COYOTE's organizational documents are literally thousands of letters from organizations, associations, and individuals inviting COYOTE representatives to speak, including the American Institute of Hypnosis; the Canadian and American Wolf Defenders; the San Francisco Institute of Public and Urban Affairs; San Francisco's chapter of the ACLU; San Francisco's Citizen's Council for Criminal Justice; California Young Republicans; the San Francisco Barristers Club; the Fresno Press Club; the Commonwealth Club of California; the Human Rights Commission of San Francisco; the California Probation, Parole and Correctional Association; the San Francisco Department of Public Health; the YWCA; county libraries; minority community centers (e.g., women's centers, Jewish community centers); in-state and out-of-state universities; and diverse students' organizations.[3] In addition, COYOTE representatives were frequently invited to speak at academic and professional conferences,[4] as well as to appear on television and radio talk shows. These invitations usually fell under the rubric of public discussions of crime, law, sex, and/or the status of women. Along with other well-established associations and organizations, agencies such as these have also expressed their interest in and/or support for COYOTE's efforts by writing letters of encouragement and sending monetary contributions.

In addition to recruiting support for the prostitutes' rights movement through speaking engagements, St. James marshalled support for COYOTE's cause from local and national celebrities, including then California governor Jerry Brown, columnist Ed Daly, Karl Menninger, Jane Fonda, Lily Tomlin, and Gloria Steinem. Gloria Steinem, for example, sent a letter of support to COYOTE and canceled a luncheon engagement with then city supervisor Diane Feinstein in protest of Feinstein's failure to support COYOTE's campaign.

EARLY SUCCESS AND GROWTH

By 1978 COYOTE's San Francisco crusade had succeeded on a number of fronts. Largely through COYOTE's work toward specific legal reforms and the decriminalization of prostitution, the conditions for local prostitutes had improved. Specifically, the quarantining of arrested prostitutes was discontinued, public defenders began to make more serious attempts to defend women arrested for prostitution, and arrested prostitutes became eligible to take advantage of the pretrial diversion program to be released on their own recognizance.

Moreover, COYOTE's campaign succeeded in obtaining local and national recognition, which laid a foundation for a national crusade. Following COYOTE's early political gains, "street walkers and call girls began to take notice, and COYOTE began to branch out" (Kellog 1974, p. 23). An article entitled "Love's Laborers Organize" reported, "COYOTE started a ripple of sympathy [for prostitutes] across the country" (Fox 1974, p. 45). Consistent with this observation, St. James, speaking at the second Annual Hookers' Convention, concluded:

> The women in COYOTE are a little paranoid about being public, of course, but not nearly as much as two years ago. They're still wondering how I'm getting away with what I'm getting away with. How? Because I'm protected now by the public—by local neighborhood organizations, by chapters of the Business and Professional Women, by middle-aged housewives and by students—an amazing range of people. Going public gets you support. (quoted in Coleman 1975, p. 6)

By the end of 1974, COYOTE boasted a membership of over ten thousand (Metzger 1975, p. 8), and three COYOTE affiliates had emerged: Associated Seattle Prostitutes (ASP), Prostitutes of New York (PONY), and Seattle Prostitutes Against Rigid Rules Over Women (SPARROW). In addition, COYOTE chapters were in the process of organizing in San Diego, New Orleans, Des Moines, Los Angeles, and Miami.

Like COYOTE, these grass roots organizations advocated the decriminalization of prostitution as a necessary step toward the alleviation of the many abuses associated with prostitution. Their spokespeople publicly argued that prostitutes' lack of legal standing and legal recourse leaves them vulnerable to many forms of exploitation from customers and law enforcement officials alike. Moreover, they argued that the *illegality* of prostitution invites arbitrary, unfair behavior and abuse of discretionary authority by police and prosecutors, which often leads to corruption and extortion.

As the result of numerous campaigns designed to disseminate this message, the prostitutes' rights movement's earliest claims-making activity culminated in producing an image of the prostitute as a victim of laws prohibiting prostitution, which, in effect, encourages police harassment and selective enforcement of prostitution. Clearly, this image contradicts, or at least challenges, historically developed images of the prostitutes as victims of illicit, commercialized sex who are in need of legal protection.

Given that COYOTE's efforts represented an affront to the law and its representatives, the prostitutes' rights movement's early campaigns were successful in prompting a series of counterclaims. These came primarily from local city officials and law enforcement officials who were concerned with maintaining prostitution's status as a vice crime worthy of prohibition and legal intervention. The counterclaims affirmed images of prostitution anchored in associations with crime, neighborhood decay, and the hazards of commercialized sex for women who engage in such activities. These counterclaims served to generate controversy and, by extension, increase the visibility and viability of the prostitutes' rights movement. In essence, the counterclaims provided spokespeople with a public forum for the dissemination of their claims about prostitution.

The way in which COYOTE representatives undertook efforts to enhance the status of local prostitutes is clearly related to the larger sociopolitical context in which they emerged and prostitution was practiced. COYOTE and its affiliates came into being to strike down prostitution laws at a time when civil libertarians and others were already calling for the decriminalization of so-called victimless crimes. Supported by local protests, public controversy, and media attention, COYOTE's grass roots movement brought attention to the status of local prostitutes by offering claims that closely resembled others' reform-minded claims that targeted the status of victimless crimes and the improprieties in law enforcement practices in general. As described in the previous chapter, the gay and lesbian community in San Francisco had already made visible claims about the inappropriateness of the law's interference in private, consensual sex between adults. At the same time, the movement to decriminalize victimless crimes publicly questioned the value of laws prohibiting so-called victimless activities, which provided no self-defined victim or complainant.

In the early 1970s COYOTE and its supporters primarily engaged in public debate with law enforcement and legislative officials in their efforts to enhance the status of local prostitutes. In the process, COYOTE's participation in legal discourse focused on debating with city officials and law enforcement agents over the comparative value of existing laws and proposed legal reform.

It is notable that the prostitutes' rights movement targeted the legal arena and its representatives in its early years. More than any other institution, the legal world was responsible for attributing deviance and ill-repute to prostitutes, while also promoting prostitution as a social problem connected to crime and moral decay. To use Best's (1990, pp. 13–16) terminology, at this point in their history COYOTE representatives constituted "outsider claims-makers" targeting "inside claims-makers" (city officials and law enforcement agents) in an effort to reconstitute dominant images of prostitution and seek ownership of the social problem of prostitution.[5]

As subsequent chapters reveal, COYOTE's target domain has shifted as the dominant source of discourse on prostitution and attendant imputations of deviance and disregard has shifted. For example, COYOTE's national and then international crusade entailed a shift in focus when it forged a link with the contemporary women's movement by engaging in feminist discourse on violence against women and commercialized sex. This strategic and substantive shift is taken up in the next chapter.

NOTES

1. "Others" stood for the lesbian contingent of the organization. As St. James explained in a personal interview (June 3, 1989), "'Others' were the dykes, but you couldn't say the word out loud then."

2. The 1978 Annual Hookers' Ball proved to be the final one. After lengthy litigation, COYOTE lost rights to the event. Ultimately, a local events promoter was granted legal rights to the event, which was subsequently transformed into what is now known as the Exotic/Erotic Ball.

3. This list is by no means exhaustive. Instead, it is included to give the flavor of the range of groups requesting COYOTE's services.

4. Indeed, representatives of the Society for the Study of Social Problems and the American Sociological Association have extended invitations to Margo St. James to speak at their national conferences. She rejected both requests.

5. Best notes that "in contemporary America, there are three principal kinds of insider claims-makers. Most obviously, there are lobbying organizations, such as the National Rifle Association and the Sierra Club, employing paid staffs to represent the interests of their clients and/or dues paying members. Second, there are professionals, the specialists charged with handling the problem, who have responsibility for and expertise about what should be done. Finally, official agencies can be claimants. . . . All three forms usually have direct access to—and influence over—policymakers. Claims-making by insiders tends to concern new wrinkles in the familiar fabric of established social problems. . . . In contrast, claims that seek recognition for new social problems often come from those outside the polity. These claims-makers can be individuals—cranks, lone crusaders, moral entrepreneurs. Or the claims can be made by social movements, seeking to gain recognition both for their social problem and for themselves as the problem's owners. Compared to insiders, these outsiders have limited access to and little influence with policymakers" (1990, pp. 13–14).

4

COYOTE's Participation in Contemporary Feminist Discourse: Proposing Prostitution as Voluntarily Chosen Service Work

INTRODUCTION

Through coalition building and the development of ties with the contemporary women's movement, COYOTE and its emergent affiliates entered the feminist debates of the late 1970s and 1980s. In the process, COYOTE's grass roots campaign was transformed into a national and then an international crusade. Taking up where the previous chapter ended, I describe that transformation in this chapter. These campaigns produced discourse that served to press claims relevant to feminist claims, and a larger movement seeking to establish and protect women's rights.

COYOTE's participation in feminist discourse, especially through public debates on violence against women, shifted the prostitutes' rights movement away from legal discourse and located it within the parameters of contemporary feminism. This allowed COYOTE and its supporters to capitalize on the public attention being devoted to the social problem of pornography and violence against women in order to press and institutionalize claims about the rights of women to choose prostitution as a viable service occupation. COYOTE's engagement in this discourse generated a wider public audience for the movement's views, while at the same time reshaping the substance of its claims. Analytically, this chapter demonstrates how COYOTE's claims about prostitution as a social problem were shaped as a result of moving away from legal discourse and into feminist discourse in a continued effort to decriminalize prostitution and legitimate the work of prostitutes.

A NATIONAL AND AN INTERNATIONAL CRUSADE

In the late 1970s COYOTE began a national and then an international crusade to decriminalize prostitution. In 1976 while in a Kansas City municipal court observing the trial of a prostitute arrested for solicitation, St. James announced that "we feel a national campaign is a necessity. There is no way we could tackle the problem state by state. It would take too long" (Zeeck 1976, n.p.). In order to kick off a national campaign, in 1976 COYOTE held its Third Annual National Hookers Convention, also referred to as the First World Meeting of Prostitutes, in Washington, D.C. At this meeting, the formation of the first Hookers' Lobby was announced. With the theme "Ignorance Is No Excuse for the Law" the Hookers' Lobby went to Capitol Hill to lobby for a resolution calling for the decriminalization of prostitution (Palmer 1976; Volz 1976; Zeeck 1976). Formulated by COYOTE, this resolution had been presented in Brussels earlier the same year at the International Tribunal on Crimes Against Women and was supported by NOW, the ACLU, and other civil rights and women's groups. Sponsored by COYOTE, the Feminist Party, and the First International Hookers' Film Festival, this lobbying effort included delegates from fourteen states and Canada, several hundred prostitutes from the East and West Coasts, and a chartered planeload of working prostitutes and ex-prostitutes from Europe. After lobbying the Capitol, delegates visited political conventions in Kansas City and New York, where they engaged in "loiter-ins" to protest the illegality of prostitution.

In another move to nationalize its campaign, COYOTE declared itself the National Task Force on Prostitution (NTFP) in 1979. The NTFP was formed in order to establish an umbrella organization responsible for developing a network of prostitutes' rights advocacy organizations in the United States. With the formation of the NTFP, the COYOTE newsletter (*COYOTE Howls*) became the *NTFP NEWS*, but continued to bear the logo of COYOTE as well as the subtitle *COYOTE Howls*. Similarly, most COYOTE letterhead bears the insignia of the NTFP and vice versa. In essence, COYOTE and the NTFP became the same organization, while organizational labels and emblems varied, depending upon activity, context, and political moment.[1]

COYOTE made its crusade international by sending representatives to the United Nations Conference on Women held in Copenhagen in 1980. A week before the 1984 Democratic National Convention in San Francisco, COYOTE sponsored the Second Annual International Hookers' Convention, which was billed as a "Women's Forum on Prostitutes' Rights" (Dorgan 1984). This event capitalized on the media personnel in town for the Democratic National Convention to draw national and international press attention to the prostitutes' rights movement. Participants in the convention also drafted a prostitutes' right platform calling for the repeal of all laws against prostitution, protection and health care for prostitutes, taxation for prostitutes, and a code of ethics for prostitutes.

In 1985 COYOTE's international crusade continued with the formation of the International Committee for Prostitutes' Rights (ICPR) based in the Netherlands. The ICPR sponsored the World Whores' Congress in Amsterdam in 1985 and in Brussels in 1986. Founders, representatives, and members of prostitutes' rights organizations from all over the world attended these conferences. Two hundred sex workers and their invited advocates from sixteen countries attended the 1986 meeting and were provided with security guards, translators, and considerable media coverage.[2] The activities and claims from the conference were eventually published in two editions of the newsletter *World Wide Whore's News* (WWWN) and in a book entitled *The Vindication of the Rights of Whores* (Pheterson 1989).

Throughout COYOTE's national and international campaign, three propositions underlying COYOTE's crusade to reconstruct the social problem of prostitution emerged and crystallized. First, prostitution is first and foremost a work issue and thus the master concept of work should replace the master concept of crime as the fundamental stance of society toward prostitution. Moreover, it is service work that should be respected and protected like work in other legitimate service occupations. Second, most women who work as prostitutes choose to do so, even in a society where prostitution is illegal. Third, and finally, prostitution is work that people should have the right to choose. Combined, these three assertions constitute COYOTE's central challenge to contemporary understandings of prostitution as a social problem, especially dominant feminist understandings of prostitution as forced sexual slavery (Barry 1979; Overall 1992).

In the next three sections, I describe each of these types of claims in order to document a shift in the imagery produced by the claims emanating from the prostitutes' rights movement. This shift parallels COYOTE's move from a grass roots effort directed at local city officials and law enforcement agents to a national and international effort enmeshed in feminist discourse and targeting contemporary feminism.

PROSTITUTION AS SERVICE WORK

More than anything else, the notion of work is central to COYOTE's position. The image of "prostitution as work" is at the core of COYOTE's assertions and demands, regardless of where they appear. The centrality of work was made evident by COYOTE leaders St. James and Alexander in an editorial in which they express their strong reaction to traditional views of prostitution:

> A rather profound misconception that people have about prostitution is that it is "sex for sale," or that a prostitute is selling her body. In reality, a prostitute is being paid for her time and skill, the price being rather dependent on both variables. To make a great distinction between being paid for an hour's sexual services, or an hour's typing, or an hour's acting on a stage is to make a distinction that is not there. (St. James and Alexander 1977, n.p.)

Continuing with this theme, Dolores French, a self-proclaimed prostitute, author of *Working: My Life as a Prostitute* (1988), president of the Florida COYOTE, president of HIRE (Hooking Is Real Employment), and an appointee to Atlanta Mayor Andrew Young's Task Force on Prostitution, argued that the work of prostitution resembles other kinds of work women do:

> A woman has the right to sell sexual services just as much as she has the right to sell her brains to a law firm where she works as a lawyer, or to sell her creative work to a museum when she works as an artist, or to sell her image to a photographer when she works as a model or to sell her body when she works as a ballerina. Since most people can have sex without going to jail, there is no reason except old fashioned prudery to make sex for money illegal. (quoted in Henkin 1988, p. 3)

Finally, the vocabulary of work is especially pronounced in the following testimony on prostitution, which was delivered to the New York State Bar Association by the leaders of COYOTE in 1985:

> The laws against pimping (living off the earnings of a prostitute) and pandering (encouraging someone to work as a prostitute) should be repealed, to be replaced with labor laws dealing with working conditions in third-party owned and managed prostitution businesses. Commissions, a majority of whose members should be prostitutes or ex-prostitutes, including individuals who have worked on the street, in massage parlors and brothels, and for escort services, should develop guidelines for the operation of third-party owned and managed businesses, including but not limited to health and safety issues, commissions, and employer/

> employee relationships. . . . Because prostitution is illegal, women and men who work in third party run prostitution businesses have no legal status as workers. Therefore, they are unlikely to have their income and social security taxes withheld, or to be provided with health, disability, and worker's compensation insurance, sick leave, vacation pay. (St. James and Alexander 1985, p. 1)

The statements above locate the activities of prostitutes in images of service work and business. Moreover, COYOTE's claims focus upon the similarities between prostitution and other types of service work.

The prostitutes' rights movement's demand to decriminalize prostitution is, in essence, a plea to allow working relationships between prostitutes and their customers and managers (pimps) to fall outside the purview of sex crime laws. Alexander explained the value of decriminalizing voluntarily chosen prostitution:

> It could involve no new legislation to deal specifically with prostitution, but merely leave the businesses which surround prostitution subject to general civil, business, and professional codes. The problems involved in forced prostitution, such as fraud and collusion, would be covered by existing penal code provisions. (1987a, p. 209)

Clearly, this view of prostitution as service work is at odds with historical and contemporary feminist views of prostitution as a source of victimization of women, as described in detail in Chapter 2.

PROSTITUTION AS VOLUNTARILY CHOSEN WORK

Through their national and international efforts, COYOTE leaders have insisted that, contrary to popular opinion, most prostitutes voluntarily choose to engage in prostitution. COYOTE continually publicly asserts that "most women who work as prostitutes have made a conscious decision to do so, having looked at a number of work alternatives" (*COYOTE Howls* 1988, p. 1). More specifically, "only 15 percent of prostitutes are coerced by third parties" (p. 1).

Assertions about prostitution emanating from the prostitutes' rights movement force a distinction between voluntary and forced prostitution. While appearing as a guest on "The Geraldo Show," the nationally televised program, Gloria Lockett, Co-Director of COYOTE, argued the following:

> If a woman does not want to be in the life, then I advocate her getting off of the streets [and] getting out of the life. I do not think

> that prostitution is for anyone who does not want to be into it. However, there is a difference between—there are some women who want to be in prostitution and some who don't want to be in it. (Rivera 1989)

Concurring is St. James (1983), who informed the press of the purpose of COYOTE's efforts:

> To defend the rights of consenting adults to have private fornication for whatever reason, and especially the rights of women to provide the service which is demanded of them. I am not out to rehabilitate—most of the women I know do not want to change professions.

Many of COYOTE's public statements suggest a clear distinction between those who choose prostitution as a line of work and those who are forced to prostitute themselves in order to survive. This distinction is the foundation upon which many of COYOTE's claims are built.

While emphasizing that most prostitution is voluntarily chosen, representatives of the prostitutes' rights movement have repeatedly repudiated the belief that most prostitutes are forced into "the life" of prostitution and, by extension, are victimized by coercion. For example, the COYOTE charter stresses that "all prostitutes are not inert, helpless objects to whom men do an endless number of things" (*COYOTE Howls* 1988, p. 1). Similarly, in an article entitled "Prostitution: A Difficult Issue for Feminists," Alexander argued that:

> The issue of forced prostitution is often used to obscure the right of women to work as prostitutes. Therefore, it is important to discuss the issue separately. At the same time, I want to make a distinction between being forced by a third party (e.g., a pimp) to work as a prostitute, particularly where violence or deceit is used, and being forced by economic reality. Most people who work for compensation do so because they need the money—for themselves, their children. In any society, people make decisions about work based on some kind of evaluation of the options open to them. And most people choose what they perceive to be the best-paying job for their skills. It is easy for other people to judge the nature of the work, but it is up to the individual to make her or his own decision about what work to do. That being said, in the technological western countries, where most women are at least functionally literate and there is a significant array of occupational choice, about ten percent of women who work as prostitutes are

> coerced into prostitution by third parties through a combination of trickery and violence. This figure appears to be relatively constant in the United States, as reflected in studies. (1987a, p. 199)

From COYOTE's perspective, a consideration of situations wherein prostitutes choose to engage in prostitution is not only in order, it is imperative as well. As St. James argued on "The Donahue Show," "we need to demand the right of these women to opt for prostitution if that's their choice. We can't deny women a choice" (quoted in Donahue 1980). Moreover, the problems associated with "forced prostitution cannot be addressed until voluntary prostitution is legitimate" (Alexander 1987a, pp. 200–1).

A belief in the affirmation and legitimation of voluntarily chosen prostitution has anchored COYOTE's national and international crusade. At the same time (as described later in this chapter), the issue of choice, and by extension coercion, constitutes the greatest point of departure between the ideology emanating from the contemporary prostitutes' rights movement and other feminist discourse on violence against women (Barry 1979; Bell 1987; Overall 1992).

PROSTITUTION AS A CIVIL RIGHTS ISSUE

COYOTE relies upon claims that prostitution is legitimate and voluntarily chosen work as a foundation for assertions about prostitutes' civil rights. Namely, COYOTE demands recognition of prostitutes civil rights as service workers. In 1982 the California chapter of NOW adopted a COYOTE resolution that:

> affirms its support of the right of women not to be forced into prostitution, as well as affirms the right of women to choose to work as prostitutes when it is their own choice and, California NOW shall support legislation to decriminalize the voluntary aspects of adult prostitution. (Alexander 1983, p. 19)

A public statement submitted to California NOW by COYOTE elaborated on the above declaration:

> Whatever one thinks of prostitution, women have the right to make up their own minds about whether or not to work as prostitutes, and under what terms. They have the right to work as free-lance workers, just as do nurses, typists, writers, doctors, and so on. They

> also have the right to work for an employer, a third party who can take care of administration and management problems . . . they have the right to a full human existence. (Alexander 1983, p. 15)

Finally, combining claims about prostitution as work and prostitutes' rights as workers, a 1988 COYOTE newsletter asserted that:

> Prostitutes have the right to work independently, to work in small collectives, or to work for agents, they should be covered by enlightened employment policies providing paid sick leave and vacation, disability, health, and workers compensation insurance, and social security, like other employed workers. (*COYOTE Howls* 1988, p. 1)

COYOTE argues that along with the right to choose prostitution as an occupation, prostitutes must have the right not to be subject to public harassment, such as stigmatization, rape, violence, denial of health care, denial of protection by and under the law, and denial of alternative job opportunities. From this perspective, as workers prostitutes should be afforded equal protection under the law and should be free from violations of their civil rights, especially in the form of legal repression and public condemnation. Thus, the "problem of prostitution" is rendered equivalent to the "problem of civil rights," which is elaborated upon in Chapter 5.

As COYOTE pressed this image of prostitution in the late 1970s, throughout the 1980s, and into the 1990s, the prostitutes' rights movement developed increasingly close ties with contemporary feminism through coalition building and acrimonious debate. As COYOTE's representatives engaged in public dialogue with contemporary feminism over the status of prostitutes in light of violence against women as a recognizable social problem, its position became increasingly distinct and public. In large part, this was accomplished via alliance building between COYOTE and other "feminist organizations" (Martin 1990).

COALITION BUILDING IN THE 1970s AND 1980s

As part of their national campaign effort, COYOTE secured alliances with other advocacy organizations, especially women's organizations. For example, one of the first significant alliances COYOTE established with a nationally recognized women's organization was with the Wages for Housework Campaign in 1977. *The Chicago Tribune* reported that:

> Strumpets and housewives both need the power money brings . . . [and] many prostitutes are also mothers with second jobs. Last

> September in a Chicago suburb, the FBI arrested three women who were part of a $100-a-night call girl operation. Many of the hookers were housewives supplementing family incomes. (Gorner 1977, p. 2)

The Los Angeles Wages for Housework chapter also formed an alliance with COYOTE to put government and business on trial for "pimping off prostitution and pimping off all the work women do" (Wages for Housework 1977, p. 8). The coalition claimed that "an attack against prostitutes is an attack on all women" (p. 8).

Boasting a membership of twenty thousand, in 1979 COYOTE aligned itself with NOW to promote a Kiss and Tell campaign designed to strengthen lobbying efforts for the passage of the Equal Rights Amendment (ERA). The Kiss and Tell idea originated in Europe, particularly Spain and Portugal, where it had some success. In Spain this tactic was used to rid the country of its adultery laws, which had been enforced only against women. In Portugal, it was used to keep abortion and prostitution laws out of the new legal code.

COYOTE's participation in the Kiss and Tell campaign in the United States was designed to assist in a larger effort to get the ERA passed, as well as to secure public funding for abortions (Castonia 1979, p. B14). A 1979 COYOTE newsletter reported:

> COYOTE has called on all prostitutes to join the international "Kiss and Tell" campaign to convince legislators that it is in their best interest to support the decriminalization of prostitution, the Equal Rights Amendment, abortion funding, lesbian and gay rights, and all other issues of importance to women. The organizers of the campaign are urging that the names of legislators who have consistently voted against those issues, yet are regular patrons of prostitutes, be turned over to feminist organizations for their use. (*COYOTE Howls* 1979, p. 1)

Interestingly, the Kiss and Tell campaign required that prostitutes violate their own code of ethics. As *COYOTE Howls* reported, "one of the points in the prostitutes' code of ethics is that the prostitute will never divulge the name of the client" (Alexander 1979a, p. 4). However, the urgency of the passage of the ERA usurped this particular ethic.

In addition to Wages for Housework and NOW, the prostitutes' rights movement also secured affiliations with other women's organizations, ranging from the Professional Women's Organization to the Feminist Party. These affiliations were conducive to COYOTE's entrance into contemporary feminist discourse.

ENTERING CONTEMPORARY FEMINIST DISCOURSE

As documented in Chapter 2, the contemporary women's movement addresses a broad set of concerns, many of which ultimately provided a public forum for COYOTE's claims about prostitution, sexuality, and the status of women in society. Indeed, already subsumed in feminist discourse were discussions of women's sexuality, the social control of women's bodies, women's right to control their bodies, and institutionalized violence against women. Combined, these discussions provided fertile soil wherein representatives of the prostitutes' rights movement could plant their position. That is, feminists' general concerns about sex for sale and violence against women provided COYOTE and its affiliates with a vehicle through which they could develop and publicly present their analyses of prostitution and proposals for reform. By entering, engaging with, and shaping contemporary feminist discourse, the prostitutes' rights movement cemented ties with the women's movement and ensured that prostitution represented a generally difficult, as well as an occasionally divisive, dilemma for feminists (Alexander 1987a; Hobson 1987; Overall 1992; Pheterson 1989; Snider 1976; St. James and Alexander 1977).

Although NOW adopted a resolution to decriminalize prostitution in 1973, it was not until the late 1970s that NOW recognized prostitution as a legitimate, albeit difficult issue. As Jaget (1980) has documented, the women's movement in the United States had been slow to support prostitute women, and even slower still in reaching agreement on the place of prostitution in the pursuit of women's liberation. As discussed in Chapter 2, feminist discussions of violence against women, including pornography and rape, were often complicated when considered along with feminists' central commitments to freedom of choice, the right to self-determination, and the importance of women securing and maintaining control over their own bodies. Debate about the nature of the intersection between these principles, coupled with a concern with responding to violence against women, provided a ripe environment for claims emanating from the prostitutes' rights movement.

COYOTE AND VIOLENCE AGAINST WOMEN

In the process of focusing on coalition building and establishing recognition as a legitimate national civil rights organization, COYOTE entered the growing and increasingly institutionalized feminist discourse on violence against women. COYOTE's former codirector, Priscilla Alexander, was a founding member of Women Against Violence in Pornography and the Media (WAVPM), which was one of the first organizations to examine the impact of violence in the media, including pornography, on women.[3] As such, she was a strong link between COYOTE and feminist discussions of pornography and violence against women. Moreover, she has been central in making public COYOTE's claims about violence against women in general and its relationship to prostitution in particular.

Alexander has consistently argued that the decriminalization of prostitution would help reduce violence against women, especially in the form of rape and pornography. As she explained in 1979:

> The NTFP is calling on the National Organization for Women to implement its 1973 resolution calling for decriminalization by establishing a prostitution task force to put pressure on the legislature. It is important that other feminist organizations, the National Women's Political Caucus and the League of Women Voters, for example, make the issue a priority alongside of the Equal Rights Amendment, abortion, domestic violence, rape, and lesbian and gay rights. Only when women are treated equally in this society, both sexually and economically, will the tremendous abuse that women face be eliminated. (Alexander 1979b, p. 3)

COYOTE's central claim is that "the outlawing of prostitution promotes rape and violence against women" (St. James, quoted in Nielson 1979, p. 105).

In order to press the argument that the decriminalization of prostitution would alleviate violence against women, COYOTE relied upon claims about the relationship between prostitution and violence against women, especially rape and pornography. Combining claims about prostitution and rape, St. James argued the following in a speech delivered at Western Washington University:

> Prohibition [of prostitution] promotes disrespect for women, promotes violence and promotes rape. . . . If we had legalized porn and prostitution at the same time, we wouldn't be sitting on the powder keg of sex and violence we're sitting on in this country. (quoted in Reiper 1982, p. 3)

This argument was pressed further by Alexander and St. James in an editorial entitled "Prostitutes Question Porno's Legitimacy":

> What the decriminalization of pornography has done is to allow an entire industry to develop that is based on a taunting and baiting,

"look, but don't touch" philosophy that is compounded by the prohibition of prostitution. . . . Should a woman offer to put on a private, pornographic show for an undercover officer, she would be arrested for soliciting an act of prostitution. (1981, n.p.)

Finally, while addressing an Episcopal church congregation in Alameda County, California, St. James claimed that prostitution should not be isolated from pornography because present laws allow "white males to sell women's bodies, but do not allow women to sell their bodies themselves" (Anderson 1984, p. 14).

Using contemporary feminist discourse on violence against women as a national forum, the prostitutes' rights movement nationally and internationally responded to the problem of violence against women by proposing the decriminalization of prostitution as a partial solution. In the process, COYOTE representatives and their supporters contested the notion that prostitutes are necessarily victimized by impersonal and commercialized sex. By construing prostitution as nothing more and nothing less than labor, COYOTE's representatives continued to contest the degree of harm involved in prostitution by promoting the element of choice for the majority of those involved in the sex industry.

However, images of prostitutes and prostitution emanating from the prostitutes' rights movement's participation in contemporary feminist discourse did not go uncontested. Consistent with the historically developed feminist analyses of prostitutes as victimized women (as described in Chapter 2), an organized nemesis emerged to adamantly refute COYOTE's claims. Women Hurt in Systems of Prostitution Engaged in Revolt (WHISPER) in particular pressed numerous counterclaims that culminated in affirming historically dominant feminist analyses of prostitution as institutionalized international sexual slavery.

WHISPER: THE EMERGENCE OF A NEMESIS

Along with the emergence of the contemporary prostitutes' rights movement, competing images of prostitution began to surface and be affirmed within the feminist discourse on violence against women. Most prominent among these was the image of the prostitute described by Kathleen Barry in her book *Female Sexual Slavery* (1979). In this book, Barry describes women who are abducted or sold for sexual purposes and transported to the United States, West Germany, Saudi Arabia, and other countries.

Female Sexual Slavery, which has been translated into four languages, served as the basis for a 1983 United Nations report that said "prostitution is slavery" and is a grave cause for international concern (Klemesrud 1985, p. C16). Barry founded the International Feminist Network Against Female Sexual Slavery in 1983 in Rotterdam. Financed by grants from the Dutch government and the Ford Foundation, this network included women who worked with grass roots women's organizations from twenty-four countries.

WHISPER emerged in the early 1980s with the expressed intent of decriminalizing and ultimately abolishing prostitution. With its headquarters in New York City, WHISPER is an organization made up of volunteers, feminist scholars, and clergy who are concerned with saving prostitutes from the life of prostitution. Like COYOTE and its affiliates, WHISPER and its supporters stress the importance of decriminalizing prostitution. Compared to COYOTE and its supporters, however, WHISPER and its advocates offer a very different justification and analysis in support of the decriminalization of prostitution.

Representatives of WHISPER argue that prostitution must first and foremost be understood as an institution created by patriarchal structures to control and abuse women. Accordingly, representatives of WHISPER claim that no woman chooses prostitution and that all prostitutes are victims. As Sarah Wynter, editor of the WHISPER newsletter, succinctly argued:

> Prostitution isn't like anything else. Rather everything else is like prostitution, because it is a model for women's condition, for gender stratification and its logical extension, sex discrimination. Prostitution is founded on enforced sexual abuse under a system of male supremacy that is itself built along a continuum of coercion. . . . We, the women of WHISPER, reject the lie that women freely choose prostitution. (Delacoste and Alexander 1987, pp. 268–69)

From WHISPER's perspective, the fact that women live under patriarchal conditions ensures that prostitutes do not choose prostitution.

From WHISPER's point of view, the "myth of choice" is only one of many myths being supported by the views promulgated by COYOTE. Other examples include the "myth of normalcy" and the "myth of professionalization." In an article entitled "Prostitution Is Not a Profession," which also appeared in French in *La Gazette des Femmes* and in English in *Women's World*, the WHISPER newsletter reported:

> The oldest profession in the world. Is it really a profession? Does one choose to be a prostitute? Last year a dozen women and men met as international experts under the auspices of UNESCO[4] to examine the issue of prostitution. The final report of this meeting

> goes a long way to exposing the deeply embedded myths about prostitution. *Myth number one*: It's just a normal social phenomenon. Not as normal as that, say the international experts. As soon as it involves boys and children, prostitution is widely held to be unacceptable and is heavily criticized in most parts of the world. Yet female prostitution is barely mentioned. It is treated as a matter of individual behavior. *Myth number two*: Prostitutes choose to go into prostitution. Not true, says UNESCO. Research shows that children who are victims of violence (incest, rape, battering) often lose their sense of physical integrity. This loss of feeling that their body belongs to them explains why women seem to "choose" when in fact there is no choice. Women who are in situations which are economically, socially or emotionally difficult, often have very little choice and will become prostitutes where others never will. Studies from the USA show that 60–65% of prostitutes have been victims of violence. In some countries, the practices are so violent—young girls are sold, imprisoned, and tortured—that the mechanism is easy to understand. *Myth number three*: Prostitution is a profession like any other. Again UNESCO experts disagree. In the 1970s, with the second wave of feminism, many groups of prostitutes started to claim the right to organise and to defend prostitution as a free profession. The women who made up these claims later admitted publicly that they had been manipulated to do so by pimps. By setting up laws and health checks which are supposed to regulate prostitution, governments are in fact trapping women and marginalising them even more, explain the experts. The laws only make things easier for the clients and increase the profits earned from prostitution. (Tremblay 1988, p. 4)

With this view of the problem in hand, the primary objective of WHISPER is the abolition of prostitution, rather than the mere removal of laws prohibiting it.

It is not surprising that in the early 1980s a schism developed between COYOTE's outlook and other feminist analyses of prostitution, especially those exemplified by WHISPER. This schism centered on the tension between COYOTE's crusade to empower prostitutes and legitimate prostitution as work, and WHISPER's attempts to rescue prostitutes from an inherently powerless position. At the heart of the acrimony between COYOTE and WHISPER are conflicting understandings of what constitutes the social problem of prostitution. A story covering a pornography and prostitution conference in Toronto alluded to the emergent tension between these two views, as represented by St. James and Barry:

> She's [St. James] been picking her way through the complex patchwork of feminist thinking on the sex trade, censorship and female sexuality for at least 10 years. What she's selling, which some parts of the women's movement are having trouble buying, is the vision of prostitution as a viable career option. In St. James' vision, the crass marketplace [of] sexuality [and] of the female skin trade is not the problem. An advocate of decriminalization, she sees prostitution as a labour issue with poor working conditions, an absence of collective bargaining rights and hostile legislators as its key determinants. And while many anti-porn feminists are sympathetic to their hooker sisters and offer resources from the women's community to fight laws which hound them, they are having trouble swallowing COYOTE's appeal to artisanal pride in the craft of commercial sex. There are subtle nuances to the debate but the counter to St. James' professionalism is a view which sees pornography as the imagery of women's subordination to men, and prostitution as its enactment. The historic feminist identity with women of the night has traditionally been constructed out of empathy for the desperate victims of harsh socio-economic realities. But increasingly, voices in the sex industry are offering an alternative perspective—one that sees prostitutes as active agents in their vocation choice. Depending on one's point of view, selling female sex is either pandering to male supremacy or a process of self-actualization whose coordinates are economic independence. (Kirzner 1985, n.p.)

Through reports such as these, the tension-filled relationship between COYOTE and WHISPER has been aired publicly. At the same time, the contest over ownership of the social problem of prostitution has grown more vehement.

Members of COYOTE have been quick to refute analyses and images of prostitution exemplified and promulgated by WHISPER's effort. St. James reacted to WHISPER-like analyses of prostitution when she claimed the following in a personal interview (June 20, 1989):

> It has nothing at all to do with reality and they're totally forgetting the people and not listening to them. And when they say working prostitutes are brainwashed [into prostitution]. I mean they totally belittle and take a super-patronizing attitude.

Repudiations such as these got aired publicly as well. For example, after attending a conference supported by the Dutch government on sexual slavery, St. James embedded COYOTE's claims in conflict with WHISPER's agenda:

> I recently travelled to the Netherlands to participate in a conference on sexual slavery by the Dutch Government—since the U.S. would never fund such a thing. It was organized by Kathy Barry, author of *Female Sexual Slavery*, a book which borders on equating slavery with prostitution. Although she gives lip service to decriminalization, she finds it impossible to grant it a professional status equal to her own. (St. James 1980, p. 7)

Similarly, Gail Pheterson, the Co-Director of the International Committee on Prostitutes' Rights (ICPR), alluded to WHISPER's efforts when she asserted that "in trying to stop abuses in prostitution, one should not try to put the women out of work" (quoted in Henkin 1989, p. 5).

The emergence of an organized ideological nemesis fueled COYOTE's crusade by generating controversy within the women's movement in particular and among the players in contemporary prostitution politics more generally. Like those debating the larger issue of pornography as sex for sale, spokespeople advocating competing views of prostitution became increasingly divided. For example, in 1985 an article appearing in the *New York Times* reported on Kathleen Barry and tension with COYOTE:

> Kathleen Barry is a soft-spoken Brandeis University sociologist whose first concern as a feminist was rape—she was a co-author of the first Stop Rape Handbook in 1972. "In those days," she said, "I thought nothing could be worse than rape." Then she heard about the international traffic in women for forced prostitution around the world. Today, the 43-year old Miss Barry is one of the recognized experts on the subject, and her goal is the eradication of forced prostitution around the world. . . . Miss Barry said one of the biggest problems she faces in her work is "the happy hooker" image, which she believes tends to glorify prostitution and make it seem like an alternative work experience. "The Xaviera Hollanders of the world only represent about 5 percent of the prostitute population," she said, quoting from her research. "More often, prostitutes are runaways who become pimp-controlled, and pimp-controlled prostitution is female sexual slavery." Asked about Margo St. James, who heads Coyote, a San Francisco-based organization that defends prostitutes' rights, she replied, "Margo was very helpful in providing information about women being victimized and exploited by police. But we basically disagree, because I want to end prostitution, and she regards it as a viable profession." (Klemesrud 1985)

Reports such as this made public the controversy surrounding COYOTE's crusade and opposition to its claims. More importantly, the emergence of organized opposition and controversy ensured that COYOTE's claims had an audience, both within the women's movement and in front of the public.

MERGING OF ADVERSARIAL FEMINIST VIEWS

The prostitutes' rights movement was quick to capitalize on the public forum and the national audience created by contemporary feminism's efforts to define rape, pornography, and prostitution as a recognizable social problem. The previous success of the antipornography campaigns in particular provided the prostitutes' rights movement with a national political forum for the dissemination of their claims about sex for sale in general and prostitution in particular. In the process of capitalizing on and joining this larger public discussion, the prostitutes' rights movement was able to reach beyond condemning the laws prohibiting prostitution and the technical aspect of the enforcement of criminal laws governing prostitution.

While COYOTE's grass roots campaigns of the early and mid-1970s sought to redefine the source of prostitutes' victimization by challenging existing legal discourse, it was COYOTE's national and international crusade that solidified a genuinely alternative conception of prostitution. Coinciding with the increasing visibility of the antipornography campaigns in the women's movement, representatives from the prostitutes' rights movement consistently packaged their claims as direct challenges to contemporary feminism. In particular, the prostitutes' rights movement targeted and responded to feminist claims about the way in which sex for sale and endemic violence against women are interrelated problems. In so doing, the prostitutes' rights movement found a home in institutionalized feminist discourse throughout the late 1970s and 1980s.

As the prostitutes' rights movement exited legal discourse and entered feminist discourse, the debate over prostitution as a social problem was significantly reconfigured and intensified. By offering an alternative, but nonetheless self-proclaimed feminist position on the status of prostitution as a social problem, COYOTE and its supporters engaged in debates with their fellow feminists over the degree to which prostitution constituted voluntarily chosen service work or institutionalized sexual slavery. Relying upon an image of prostitution as voluntarily chosen service work, COYOTE pressed claims about prostitutes' civil rights as workers who are wrongly prohibited from participating in sex for sale as a line of service work—nothing more, and nothing less. At the same time, and consistent with larger concerns about violence against women, analyses emanating from contemporary feminism suggested that prostitution is neither work nor a voluntarily chosen activity. Rather, it is institutionalized forced sexual slavery resulting from patriarchal structures—nothing more, and nothing less. The nothing more and nothing less implicit in each of these perspectives constituted the core tension between COYOTE representatives and other feminist prostitutes' advocates.

Given that the increasingly visible prostitutes' rights movement represented an affront to dominant themes in contemporary feminism, it met with organized opposition. That is, the prostitutes' rights movement's national efforts were successful in prompting a series of counterclaims. Counterclaims came primarily from feminist representatives and those primarily concerned with getting women out of prostitution and abolishing the practice of prostitution. The most significant were WHISPER's nationally organized efforts to abolish prostitution and increase public awareness about the harm of sex for sale in this country and abroad. Opposition such as WHISPER's served to mark COYOTE's position as a legitimate contender in the battle to own the social problem of prostitution from a feminist perspective.

As public debates between the representatives of the prostitutes' rights movement and their feminist critics ensued, the visibility and viability of the prostitutes' rights movement was enhanced in several ways. First, the claims and counterclaims led to a crystallization of COYOTE's views. Second, they ensured that COYOTE's perspective received a wider hearing within the women's movement in particular, and among central players in the politics of prostitution more generally. Third, and perhaps most importantly, they were critical in marshalling national recognition for the prostitutes' rights movement from the press as well as numerous nemeses.

Like COYOTE's grass roots efforts, the way in which COYOTE and its supporters undertook a national effort to legitimate prostitution and normalize prostitutes is related to the larger sociopolitical context in which they maneuvered. COYOTE's national crusade emerged at the very moment when contemporary feminism was increasingly coming to own the problem of prostitution, in large part because of its ownership of the problem of violence against women. Accordingly, the prostitutes' rights movement's national efforts brought attention to the problem of prostitution by offering claims that attended closely to the larger and much more established issue of violence against women.

It is not surprising that the prostitutes' rights movement targeted contemporary feminism and its representatives throughout its national and international crusade. More than any other institution, contemporary feminism was increasingly responsible for attributing victimization to prostitutes, while also promoting prostitution as a social problem connected with violence against women. Similar to the way in which the legal arena was approached in the formative years of the prostitutes' rights movement, the feminist arena was relied upon in subsequent years. Namely, it was targeted as the dominant source of unacceptable constructions of prostitution as a social problem.

However, unlike the prostitutes' rights movement's consistently adversarial participation in legal discourse, its participation in feminist discourse has been characterized by acrimonious debate *and* sporadic allegiance. Insofar as COYOTE and its affiliates offered an alternative feminist position on prostitution, their efforts became fused with contemporary feminism as they merged with larger efforts to respond to violence against women. This fusion contributed to a significant shift in their standing as claims-makers. Specifically, they became increasingly recognizable as "insider claims-makers" (Best 1990, pp. 13–16). As Best describes, "claims-making by insiders tends to concern new wrinkles in the familiar fabric of established social problems" (p. 14). In this case, the "new wrinkle" is voluntarily chosen prostitution as service work, while the "familiar fabric of established social problems" is violence against women.

As the next chapter reveals, COYOTE's target arena shifts once again as the dominant source of discourse on prostitution and attendant imputations of deviance and disregard shift. This time, the AIDS epidemic serves to locate the problem of prostitution within the realm of public health discourse. Accordingly, the prostitutes' rights movement has (re)directed its attention toward this institutionalized arena of discourse and its attendant experts. And, in the process, has become even more recognizable as "inside claims-makers." This strategic and substantive shift is the topic of the next chapter.

NOTES

1. Throughout the remainder of this work, I continue to refer to this organization as COYOTE since this is the name most frequently used by the organization's leaders, as well as by the press.

2. Representatives from the following organizations figured prominently in the event: the International Prostitution Documentation Center and ASPASIE, Geneva; Prostitution Laws Are Nonsense (PLAN) and the English Collective of Prostitutes (ECP), both of Great Britain; Comitato per i Diritti Civili delle Prostitute (Committee for the Civil Rights of Prostitutes), Italy; HYDRA, Berlin; HWG, Frankfurt; Solidarietaet Hamburger Huren (Solidarity of Hamburg

Whores), Hamburg; Messalina, Munich; Kassandra, Nuremberg; Lysistrata, Cologne; Nitribitt, Bremen; Canadian Organization for Prostitutes (CORP); the Australian Prostitutes Collective; the Austrian Association of Prostitutes; De Rode Draad (the Red Thread) and De Roze Draad (the Pink Thread), the Netherlands; and the National Association of Prostitutes, Brazil.

3. It is important to note that there have been dramatic shifts in Alexander's analyses of the relationship between prostitution and violence against women since undertaking her work with COYOTE. Alexander informed me in a letter (February 22, 1990) that "I am adamantly opposed to the policies [of Women Against Violence Against Women in Pornography and Media (WAVAW]) and much of the analysis of the 'radical' feminist anti-pornography movement."

4. United Nations Education, Scientific and Cultural Organization.

5

COYOTE's Participation in Public Discourse on AIDS: Countering Assertions that Prostitutes Represent Pools of Contagion

INTRODUCTION

The AIDS epidemic represents the most recent and the most dramatic change in the political environment of prostitutes' rights organizations. By the mid 1980s, the AIDS epidemic posed a recognizable health, social, and legal threat to prostitutes. As such, it represents a significant environmental constraint to the prostitutes' rights movement. As a result, COYOTE and other sex workers' organizations have responded to the AIDS epidemic with considerable organizational activity.

This chapter brings COYOTE's crusade into the 1990s by focusing on the ways in which the AIDS epidemic has affected the evolution of the contemporary prostitutes' rights movement in general, and its claims-making activities in particular. My focus is on the prostitutes' rights movement's efforts to respond to the many environmental constraints posed by the AIDS epidemic. Specifically, COYOTE's recent efforts to shape public perceptions around the ways in which prostitutes have been "scapegoated" for the spread of AIDS have replaced the many political activities undertaken by the movement prior to being confronted with AIDS. In order to explain this shift in organizational agenda and subsequent social movement trajectory, this chapter briefly describes AIDS as a social problem, as well as a health, social, and legal threat to prostitutes. Then the remainder of the chapter examines COYOTE's response to the AIDS crisis, as well as how this response has affected the evolution of its crusade to decriminalize and legitimate prostitution.

AIDS AS A SOCIAL PROBLEM

Theoretical and empirical work has examined how AIDS has been constructed as an identifiable social problem (Albert 1986, 1989; Altman

1986; Fettner and Check 1985; Patton 1990). In many ways, the evolution of AIDS resembles the social construction of other diseases such as leprosy, syphilis, tuberculosis, and cholera (Rosenberg 1962; Sontag 1977; Volinn 1983). In each of these epidemics, the evolution of the disease was not only tied to the biological characteristics of the disease, but was a result of the socially constructed definition(s) of the disease as well.

From the beginning, many claims-makers have sought to make their interpretations of the AIDS epidemic dominant. Driven by a variety of concerns, scientists, physicians, afflicted groups, government agencies, and other claims-makers concerned with the disease were quick to formulate and disseminate interpretations of the disease along numerous dimensions. The media became a primary arena through which many individuals and organizations sought to have their claims disseminated to and ultimately adopted by the public. Thus, the media have played a central role in the construction of AIDS as a social problem (Albert 1986, 1989).

Although the media were slow to cover AIDS, once the issue finally became a story, the "mysterious killer evolved into a disease of deviant sexuality" (Albert 1989, p. 51). As a way of accounting for the disease and the epidemic the press focused not so much on the disease itself, but on groups whose life-style made them susceptible to AIDS. By focusing on the sociocultural characteristics of homosexual men, the largest epidemiological group affected by AIDS, the press concentrated on the details of their life-style, claiming that it caused the spread of AIDS. By adopting a dual focus on deviant life-styles and the medical problem of AIDS, press coverage of AIDS tied the medical problem to a moral issue.

Throughout the early eighties, AIDS was popularly understood as a fatal disease associated with homosexuality, intravenous drug use, and promiscuous sex. Since AIDS was first observed in individuals whose life-style made the transfer of blood, blood products, or bodily fluids relatively likely, first homosexual men and later intravenous drug users were identified as "at risk" groups. As a result, the disease was tied to behavior defined as deviant and individuals defined as deviants (Albert 1986, 1989; Fettner and Check 1985).

By 1985, however, AIDS was beginning to be understood as an explicit threat to the heterosexual population. As Albert explained:

> By the fall of 1985, AIDS was spreading into the consciousness of Americans, not so much as an illness, but as an idea that was increasingly affecting the way Americans experienced daily life. Thus, the press redefined AIDS. One now had to view AIDS as an

> inescapable feature of day-to-day life. . . . In short, AIDS spread into the consciousness of American journalism and, by extension, into the consciousness of the American public. (1989, p. 47)

As the "gay plague" entered the "general population," the AIDS epidemic was constructed as a fundamentally different type of social problem. Portrayed as a threat to the population at large, AIDS became a disease of the "normal" as well as a disease of the "deviant."

As media attention turned to the emergent heterosexual threat, it began to focus on the issue of contagion with the same fervor it had previously focused on the life-styles of those infected. As the danger of AIDS to heterosexuals attracted more media attention, the AIDS epidemic was redefined as a problem facing school children, married women, college students, and prison inmates. At the same time, concerns about halting the disease were heightened. For example, it was not until the heterosexual threat was constructed and recognized that Surgeon General Koop called for AIDS preventive education in the public schools across the nation.

Nonetheless, AIDS has not lost its original connection with deviants, deviant life-styles, and promiscuous sex. The disease has been continually constructed as one implicating deviants in general and sexual deviants in particular. In this way, prostitutes too have been implicated in the AIDS epidemic.

IMPLICATING PROSTITUTES

The biological characteristics of AIDS, combined with the way in which the disease has been socially constructed, almost ensured that prostitutes would be implicated in the social problem of AIDS. In an article entitled "Prostitutes and AIDS: Public Policy Issues," Cohen, Alexander, and Wofsy concluded that "prostitutes have often been held responsible for the spread of AIDS into the heterosexual population in this country" (1988, p. 16). This is not particularly surprising given that AIDS has been primarily conceived as a sexually transmitted disease, and that the historical association of prostitution with venereal disease, promiscuous sex, and moral unworthiness remains fixed in the minds of the public (Brandt 1985; du Plessix Gray 1992; Hobson 1987; Pheterson 1986; Sheehy 1974).

Prostitutes have been implicated in the AIDS epidemic as a primary bridge through which AIDS has been transmitted into the heterosexual population, and by 1984 medical authorities were actively investigating that possibility. At the same time, the media contributed to making prostitution suspect as an avenue of transmission for the disease. For example, on a 1989 episode of the nationally televised "The Geraldo Show" entitled "Have Prostitutes Become the New Typhoid Marys?" the host offered the following introduction to millions of viewers:

> The world's oldest profession may very well have become among its deadliest. A recent study backed by the federal Centers for Disease Control found that one third of New York's prostitutes now carry the AIDS virus. If this study mirrors the national trend, then the implications are as grim as they are clear. Sleeping with a prostitute may have become a fatal attraction. . . . A quick trick may cost you twenty dollars, but you may be paying for it with the rest of your life. (Rivera 1989)

Supporting Rivera's introduction, a New York–based AIDS counselor appearing on the show argued:

> A high percentage of prostitutes infected with HIV pass it on to their sexual partners who are johns or the tricks, a lot of whom are married or have sex with a straight woman. I think this is how the AIDS epidemic is passed into the heterosexual population. (Cristallo 1989)

He argued further that working prostitutes testing positive for the human immunodeficiency virus (HIV) are guilty of manslaughter and/or attempted murder. In a relatively short period of time, claims such as this have become commonplace.

THE EMERGENCE OF LEGISLATION

Throughout history, prostitution has been portrayed as a health threat as well as a moral threat. Many social historians have documented that, especially during the nineteenth century, female sexual organs, particularly those of prostitutes, were associated with disease and decay (Brandt 1987; du Plessix Gray 1992; Walkowitz 1980, 1983). For example, in the first half of the twentieth century "physicians and social reformers associated venereal disease, almost exclusively, with the vast population of prostitutes in American cities" (Brandt 1987, p. 31). The association between prostitution and disease has left prostitutes vulnerable to increased social control, primarily in the form of state regulation (Bergman 1988; Brandt 1987).

Thus, it is not particularly surprising that legislators have once again turned their attention to prostitution as an avenue of transmission for an epidemic. In the name of preventing the transmission of the HIV infection, legislation that intrudes into private, consensual sexual relations has sprung up around the country. A number of proposals have been introduced that would, in one way or another, make it a crime for someone who is HIV positive to engage in sex with anyone else, regardless of the degree to which the behavior is mutually voluntary and whether or not condoms are used (Luxenberg and Guild 1990). At the same time, jurisdictions that have no AIDS-specific criminal law have begun to rely on traditional criminal laws (e.g., attempted murder, aggravated assault) to prosecute HIV-positive individuals who engage in behaviors that put seronegative individuals at risk.

The introduction of AIDS-related legislation has posed a legal threat to prostitutes. Many governmental and medical establishments have reacted to AIDS with calls for increased regulation of prostitution in the form of registration, mandatory AIDS testing, and prison sentences for those carrying antibodies to the virus. In the mideighties and into the nineties, many states considered legislation requiring that arrested prostitutes be tested for HIV infection. Most of the proposed statutes make those who test positive subject to arrest on felony charges.

As early as 1988, many states had introduced legislation requiring mandatory testing of arrested prostitutes. Specifically, Georgia, Florida, Utah, and Nevada were the first states legislating the forcible testing of arrested prostitutes. The mandatory testing laws, in effect, create a state registry of infected prostitutes. At the same time, the felony charges could create a quarantine situation if prostitutes are kept in isolation while awaiting trial.

Coinciding with the introduction of legislation, many judges and district attorneys began contemplating and occasionally charging arrested prostitutes who tested positive for HIV with attempted manslaughter and murder. In July 1990, for example, an Oakland, California, prostitute was arrested after *Newsweek* ran a photo of her and quoted her as saying she had contracted the deadly virus from contaminated needles but continued to engage in prostitution. According to newspaper reports, Oakland police asked a judge to force the woman to be tested for AIDS and pressured the district attorney's office to pursue an attempted manslaughter charge if she tested positive (*Sacramento Bee* 1990, p. B7). Although the judge denied the charge, the woman was held for a number of days while the possibility of pursuing the charge was contemplated. In another case, in Orlando, Florida, an HIV-infected prostitute was charged with manslaughter even though she had used a condom with all of her clients, and despite the finding that all of her clients who had been tested were found to be HIV negative (Alexander 1988).

There are many such examples, and the conclusion is clear: The AIDS epidemic has led to increased social control of prostitutes, especially in the form of repressive legislation and increasingly punitive legal sanctions. Such changes reflect the commonly held belief that prostitutes constitute a "vector of transmission" for AIDS into the heterosexual population. Although some have suggested that the introduction and implementation of AIDS-related statutes is merely an attempt to mollify public fear of AIDS spreading into the population at large (Leigh 1987, 1988; Luxenberg and Guild 1990), legislation and increased legal sanctions have nonetheless been pursued by public officials and activists alike in the name of controlling the spread of AIDS.

THE SCAPEGOATING OF PROSTITUTES FOR AIDS

Not surprisingly, prostitutes' rights organizations and their representatives were quick to respond to the multitude of threats posed by AIDS, as well as public officials' response to the epidemic. As early as 1984, when prostitutes met at the Second Annual International Hookers' Convention:

> More than political theories, the hookers wanted to discuss actual practices, and AIDS was very much on their minds. Advice was exchanged as to how to avoid the often-fatal disease. For example, avoid oral-anal sex; don't share sex toys. (Mitchell 1984, p. 10)

In addition to sharing information on how to prevent the contraction and transmission of AIDS, in the mideighties prostitutes and their advocates focused on the threat of being implicated in the transmission of the disease. As COYOTE Co-Director Lockett explained, "prostitutes are traditionally used as symbols of immoral sexuality, and are the first scapegoats of the forces of moral repression" (quoted in Winklebleck 1988, p. 2).

Many of COYOTE's more recent claims-making activities are in direct response to the popular notion that prostitutes represent a social problem because they constitute a threatening avenue for the transmission of AIDS into the general population. In a press release entitled "Women and AIDS/Prostitutes and AIDS," COYOTE made explicit the popular conceptualization of prostitution as a health problem connected to AIDS:

> Women who are infected with HIV or who have been diagnosed with AIDS are viewed as "vectors" for the transmission of AIDS to men or to children, not as people who get the disease and need

> services. Symbolic of this view is the frequent categorization of female prostitutes—in Africa, in Asia, in the United States—as "pools of contagion" or "reservoirs of infection." (*COYOTE Howls* 1988, p. 1)

Similarly, Carol Leigh, an outspoken COYOTE member and spokeswoman, argued the following in an editorial aptly entitled "AIDS: No Reason for a Witchhunt": "Prostitutes become like other vulnerable victims of society, scapegoats and targets of backlash against this disease and the people who have it. Misfortune always hits hardest at those on the bottom" (1987, p. 1). In response to prostitutes being viewed as deadly pools of contagion, COYOTE has undertaken numerous campaigns to dismantle the conceptualization of prostitutes as contractors, carriers, and transmitters of the virus.

COYOTE counters conceptualizations of prostitutes as pools of contagion by construing such assertions as the political scapegoating of stigmatized, thus vulnerable, populations. For example, as part of the Sex Workers/Outlaws in Civil Disobedience contingent of the National March on Washington for Lesbian and Gay Rights in 1987, COYOTE and its supporters pressed the following analysis:

> During the AIDS crisis populations with little power, societal acceptance or political representation are extremely vulnerable to social and legislative scapegoating. Prostitutes are the most obvious targets of those who wish to control the sexual behavior of the general population, often serving as symbols of promiscuity and illicit sex and disease. (*Civil Disobedience Handbook* 1987, p. 1)

Consistent with the politics of other minority groups, COYOTE construes the AIDS crisis as one that has led to the political scapegoating of prostitutes (Alexander 1987b; Pheterson 1989). As Pheterson, the co-director of the International Committee on Prostitutes' Rights (ICPR) succinctly explained in the introduction to *The Vindication of the Rights of Whores*:

> The AIDS epidemic has reached alarming proportions and prostitutes are being scapegoated for spreading the disease. Like a hundred years ago during the syphilis epidemic, many governmental and medical establishments reacted to AIDS with increased regulation of prostitution (e.g., registration, mandatory AIDS testing and even prison sentences for those carrying antibodies to the virus). . . . Unlike a hundred years ago, prostitutes in many countries are responding publicly on their own behalf. (1989, p. 28)

COYOTE substantiates its assertions about prostitutes being scapegoated for the spreading of AIDS by pressing claims about prostitutes' differential HIV infection rates and by underscoring the civil rights violations involved in the forced testing of prostitutes.

PRESSING CLAIMS ABOUT HIV INFECTION RATES

COYOTE has countered assertions that prostitutes represent a pool of contagion by suggesting that prostitutes' rates of HIV infection are lower than other demographic groups. In the process, spokespeople for the prostitutes' rights movement invoke the use of many scientific studies and researchers to lend legitimacy to their claims. For example, ex-prostitute and COYOTE codirector Gloria Lockett claimed the following at a press conference in 1988: "Prostitutes test no higher for exposure to HIV than other women—when studies take into consideration IV drug use—since prostitutes use condoms" (quoted in Winklebleck 1988, p. 2). Similarly, at the Second World Whores Congress and in the ICPR newsletter *World Wide Whores News,* the following was announced:

> AIDS researchers have confirmed that the kind of sexual activities and not the number of sex partners is critical to AIDS risk. Prostitutes are not more likely than other women to practice unsafe sex; in fact, as professionals, many prostitutes are better informed and more cautious. (1985, p. 3)

In addition to asserting prostitutes' comparatively low infection rates, COYOTE has publicly explained that sex workers are not at risk for AIDS because of prostitution per se; viruses do not discriminate between those who exchange money for sex and those who do not. As the codirector of the ICPR claimed in her book *A Vindication of the Rights of Whores* in 1989:

> They [prostitutes] are demanding the same medical confidentiality and choice as other citizens. . . . They are contesting policies which separate them from other sexually active people, emphasizing that charging money for sex does not transmit disease. (Pheterson 1989, p. 28)

COYOTE's media legislative coordinator concurred in a guest editorial appearing in the *Oakland Tribune* in 1987:

> Many readers are well aware that prostitutes practice safe sex techniques, using condoms for oral services as well as intercourse, and

> quite often restricting their activities to manual gratification. Many prostitutes emphasize massage, still others combine fantasy stimulation (S&M, etc.) with minimal physical contact. There is much a "working girl" can do to assure her health and the health of her clients, and we have done it. Most of us followed safe sex practices long before the onset of this epidemic. (Leigh 1987, p. 1)

Finally, in an article entitled "Prostitutes Are Being Scapegoated for Heterosexual AIDS," Alexander explained:

> Prostitutes have always been quite concerned about sexually transmitted diseases. . . . Therefore, prostitutes have tended to be quite responsible about being checked for diseases to protect themselves, as well as to protect others. They quickly learn to recognize the symptoms of sexually transmitted diseases in men and refuse to have sexual contact with men they believe to be infected. Prostitutes have always made use of prophylactic measures that have been available. . . . This caution has only increased since the outbreak of AIDS. (1987b, p. 203)

Claims similar to those described above culminate in suggestions that prostitutes, especially street prostitutes, practice safe sex, get regular health checks, and insist that clients wear condoms. From COYOTE's perspective, prostitutes do *not* constitute an "at risk" group because, at least in part, they have always been cautious about sexually transmitted diseases out of concern for their own health and their ability to work. By extension, what separates prostitutes from "women in general" is *higher* rates of condom use.

Related to this, COYOTE accounts for prostitutes who have tested positive for the HIV infection by pointing to intravenous drug use among some prostitutes. COYOTE concedes that to the extent that prostitutes have become infected, their rate of infection has paralleled the rate among intravenous drug users in their communities. As Lockett (1989) argued on "The Geraldo Show":

> You're focusing mostly on prostitutes when you should be focusing on drug use—not on prostitution. All of the prostitutes—almost every one of them—that were positive in her [another guest, Dr. Joyce Wallace] study were IV drug users or crack-using prostitutes. *That* is the problem.

COYOTE's claims suggest that prostitutes who have tested positive in seroprevalence studies or who have been diagnosed with AIDS have a history of intravenous drug use. As explained in *COYOTE Howls*:

> Prostitutes have been scapegoated for heterosexual AIDS since it was first realized the disease was sexually transmitted. However, numerous studies have found that prostitutes are not at risk for AIDS, unless they use IV drugs themselves (and share unsterile needles), or have unprotected sex with a man who uses IV drugs. (1988, p. 2)

Similarly, Alexander reported:

> There have been a number of studies of the rate of infection with the AIDS virus among prostitutes, and it appears that four or five percent of the prostitutes in the United States, most of them IV drug users or lovers of IV users, have the antibodies to the virus. (1987b, p. 203)

Through claims such as these, the focus on prostitutes and prostitution as vectors of disease is purported to be misguided, while a distinction between drug-using and non-drug-using prostitutes is enforced.

OPPOSING MANDATORY TESTING

In addition to promoting the notion that prostitutes do not represent a pool of contagion, COYOTE has distributed public announcements, attended conferences, issued press releases, and staged protests to oppose legislation requiring the mandatory testing of prostitutes for the AIDS virus. COYOTE has protested on the grounds that selective forced testing is discriminatory and thus a violation of individuals'—in this case prostitutes'—civil rights. As Alexander explained in an article entitled "A Chronology of Sorts":

> By the spring of 1983, AIDS began to pose serious problems for lesbians, gay men, bisexuals, and other sexually stigmatized groups, by setting the stage for major civil rights violations. . . . I figured prostitutes would in some way become involved. (1988, p. 169)

In agreement was the current Co-Director of COYOTE, who argued that "they [prostitutes] should not be targeted for measures which so patently violate our civil rights" (Lockett quoted in Winklebleck 1988, p. 2).

Many of COYOTE's recent protests are in direct response to the threat of mandatory testing of AIDS legislation. A San Francisco paper reported on a local protest staged by COYOTE and its supporters:

> Outraged members of COYOTE, a national organization concerned with the rights of male and female prostitutes, sent up a howl in San Francisco last week at the recent passage of two state bills aimed at putting prostitutes who test HIV positive behind bars. . . . Earlier this year COYOTE joined ranks with AIDS activists ACT UP and the US Prostitutes Collective to protest the proposed legislation before Speaker of the House Willie Brown and other politicians and lobbyists in Sacramento. They argued that the proposals singled out and unfairly punished a group which tests HIV positive no more frequently than do other sexually active women in the United States. "Prostitutes haven't been transmitting AIDS," asserted Carol Leigh (a.k.a. Scarlot Harlot), COYOTE legislative media coordinator. "Most of the prostitutes I know are getting tested on their own. They use condoms. Obviously we're being used as a symbol." (Everett 1988, n.p.)

Newspaper editorials and press reports reiterate the theme that mandatory testing is a violation of individuals' civil rights, including those of prostitutes. For example, in response to the introduction of a series of state bills targeting mental patients, prisoners, and prostitutes for mandatory AIDS testing, including one to repeal the guarantee of confidentiality of AIDS tests, a COYOTE spokeswoman offered the following plea in a 1987 guest editorial in the *Oakland Tribune*:

> Mandatory testing for the AIDS virus has been discredited by almost the entire medical establishment as counterproductive in the battle against the disease. . . . [However,] these plans are promoted by our president and legislators who say they want to reduce the public's fear of contamination by the undesirables of our society. On the surface, mandatory testing of prostitutes and prisoners sounds like it makes sense, representing an effort to control "lawbreakers." But, if we look below the surface, we see people who are already victimized by unfair laws and the discriminatory enforcement of them: gays, prostitutes, and people of color. As a prostitute I am familiar with the injustice that results from this kind of stigma and prejudice. It is imperative that anyone who espouses fairness and the protection of civil rights pay diligent attention to these most vulnerable members of society, people who cannot often speak for themselves. . . . We must remain alert to violations and intended violations of human rights. We must work to reclaim and protect the rights of gays, persons with AIDS/ARC, prostitutes (and other sex workers), prisoners, IV drug users, poor people and people of color. (Leigh 1987, p. 1)

Remarks such as these remain fairly consistent with the advocacy work of other minority groups protesting on their own behalf in light of the AIDS epidemic. Like these other groups, COYOTE protests the implementation of mandatory AIDS testing on the grounds that it is a violation of individuals' rights, especially the right to privacy.

The prostitutes' rights movement's AIDS-related claims also point to the selective nature of mandatory testing as further evidence of civil rights violations. At a press conference held to discuss a mandatory testing bill that passed both houses of the California legislature, Gloria Lockett stated: "If, in the name of public health, there is to be a law against people who are HIV positive having sex, let it apply to everyone, not just the most politically vulnerable group [prostitutes]" (quoted in Winklebleck 1988, p. 2). COYOTE's AIDS-related claims contain themes of their earlier claims about the law and its selective enforcement as the source of prostitutes' victimization and prostitution as a civil rights issue. However, the urgency of pressing AIDS-related claims required a circumvention of the movement's original primary goal(s). As Alexander explained in a personal interview while describing the effect that the AIDS epidemic has had on COYOTE: "We [COYOTE] don't have time for focusing a concerted effort on decriminalization, we're worried about quarantining [of prostitutes]" (September 21, 1988).

SHIFT IN FOCUS AND CIRCUMVENTION OF GOALS

It is not uncommon for social movement organizations to modify, transform, and occasionally even to subvert the objectives for which they were originally established. Occasionally, they abandon the goals for which they were originally created, and adopt goals that facilitate the immediate and/or long-range survival of the organizations. In the latter part of the 1980s, COYOTE constituted an instance of this sort of organizational goal displacement. Namely, there was a demonstrable shift away from COYOTE's original primary goal of decriminalizing prostitution to a focus on responding to the scapegoating of prostitutes for AIDS, and by extension, on combatting the increased social control of prostitution. Obviously, this shift in focus and goals has had a significant impact on the types of activities that COYOTE has come to sponsor in the latter part of the 1980s and into the 1990s.

AIDS education efforts have taken primacy as the substantive organizational goal of COYOTE, even as it still advocates the decriminalization of prostitution. The primacy of AIDS-related activity is evident by numerous indicators, including a change in COYOTE's leadership in the mideighties, a change in the organization's charter and recruitment, the prevalence of AIDS-related information in COYOTE's press releases and publications, the emergence and implementation of the California Prostitutes' Education Program (CAL-PEP), and Priscilla Alexander's move to the World Health Organization.

Change in Leadership

In 1986 St. James moved to France to work through the ICPR. The *San Francisco Chronicle* reported a change in the leadership of COYOTE, which reflected the organization's emerging concern with AIDS:

> When Margo St. James moves to Europe at the end of March, she will leave behind her Rolodex. The Rolodex is nothing like your Rolodex. Yours probably lists the usual business associates, your accountant, the dentist and your favorite Indian restaurant. Hers has numbers for cops, hookers and pimps, feminists and gays, Catholic nuns, Franciscan brothers, sociologists, shrinks, doctors, lawyers, churches and schools, the mayor's office. . . . St. James, the founder of COYOTE, a prostitutes' trade union, will turn everything over to Priscilla Alexander, a feminist educator, and Gloria Lockett, a former prostitute. . . . The teaming of feminist and hooker pleases St. James, who founded COYOTE (Call Off Your Old Tired Ethics) 15 years ago. Her main intent has been to get rid of what she views as archaic anti-prostitution laws and gain societal acceptance for women in the sex industry. . . . St. James can't think of a better duo than Alexander and Lockett to take her job. . . . Lockett, who was a working prostitute for 19 years, joined COYOTE in 1982, leading rap and support groups for prostitutes and educating them on AIDS prevention. . . . Lockett quit working the streets a couple of years ago, mainly because of her age (she is 39). She [now] works four days a week at Project Aware, a non-profit research staff affiliated with the University of San Francisco and San Francisco General Hospital, which is surveying women (both prostitutes and non-prostitutes) to determine what puts them at risk of getting AIDS. . . . Alexander's main concern is educating the public about prostitution and AIDS. Prostitutes are always linked in the public's mind with the spread of disease, she said. "But there isn't any documented evidence of a customer getting AIDS from a prostitute." . . . As for St. James, she is picking up French by watching foreign films on her VCR, and has already started a new Rolodex. "With me out of the way, COYOTE might grow in a way it couldn't before." (Rubin 1986, n.p.)

The departure of St. James, coupled with the arrival of Lockett and Alexander, signaled and reflected a shift in COYOTE's priorities and concerns. Namely, the organization turned away from advocacy work surrounding the decriminalization of prostitution and toward public education around the AIDS epidemic.

Change in Organizational Charter and Recruitment

Consistent with this change in leadership, COYOTE spokespeople began to identify COYOTE as an organization primarily concerned with responding to the many threats posed by the AIDS epidemic. A 1988 charter explicitly stated COYOTE's primary concern:

> COYOTE is working to prevent the scapegoating of prostitutes for AIDS and other sexually transmitted diseases, and to educate prostitutes, their clients, and the general public about prevention of these diseases. (*COYOTE Howls* 1988, p. 1)

As COYOTE's charter changed to reflect a concern with the politics of AIDS, so too did its membership. COYOTE and its affiliates now explicitly recruit individuals concerned with the welfare of prostitutes in particular and the spread of AIDS in general. As Carol Leigh declared while trying to recruit members in 1987, "these days we're mostly involved in safe sex education" (Harlot 1987, n.p.).

AIDS Information in Press Releases and Publications

No later than the summer of 1985, COYOTE began focusing on the social problem of AIDS full force, often almost exclusively. At the Second National Hookers' Convention, for example, participants spent the majority of their time discussing AIDS at great length and developing statements and policies on mandatory testing, quarantining, risk reduction measures, and the need for public education.

Consistent with the primacy of AIDS on the organizational agenda, COYOTE has increasingly used public appearances to discuss the transmission and prevention of AIDS. For example, when COYOTE representatives appeared on "The Today Show," they opposed the image of prostitutes as pools of contagion, promoted the image of prostitutes as scapegoats, and introduced the condom as the way to prevent AIDS.[1] Not only did COYOTE spokespersons openly discuss the logistics of condom use, they claim to have been responsible for the condom's debut on national television (Priscilla Alexander, personal communication, September 21, 1988).

The primacy of COYOTE's concern with AIDS is also reflected in its more recent press releases and publications. In the main, COYOTE's newsletters from 1986 to the present constitute reports on AIDS-related legislation, analyses of the scapegoating of prostitutes for AIDS, and requests for volunteers interested in bringing a halt to AIDS in general and the blaming of prostitutes in particular. COYOTE's January 1989 newsletter, for example, offered exclusive coverage of the AIDS epidemic, including AIDS laws affecting prostitutes that were passed in California in 1989 (*Coyote Howls* 1989). This preoccupation is also obvious in other prostitutes' rights newsletters both in the United States and abroad (e.g., *The Oldest Profession Times* and *Horizontal*).

The Emergence and Implementation of CAL-PEP

The primacy of AIDS-related concerns has been most visible through the emergence and implementation of CAL-PEP. In 1987 COYOTE was asked by the AIDS Activity Office of the California Department of Health to submit a proposal for an AIDS prevention project for prostitutes. As a result, CAL-PEP was awarded a thirty-thousand-dollar grant, which was increased to fifty thousand dollars within the first year, for the purpose of educating street prostitutes about safer sex practices and intravenous drug use hygiene.

CAL-PEP currently operates out of COYOTE's main office in San Francisco, shares personnel with COYOTE, and uses COYOTE's letterhead and logo. As CAL-PEP's statement of purpose sheet explains:

> CAL-PEP, the California Prostitutes Education Project, is an education project developed by members of COYOTE, the prostitutes' rights advocacy organization, to provide educational programs for prostitutes and the interested public on various aspects of prostitution. Our first project is an AIDS prevention project designed and implemented by prostitutes, ex-prostitutes, and prostitutes' rights advocates to help prostitutes to protect themselves and their clients from AIDS. (Schlesinger Library Holdings, n.d.)

CAL-PEP outreach workers go into the "stroll districts" where street prostitutes work, and they distribute condoms, spermicides, bleach bottles, and educational materials, and talk to prostitutes about how they can work safely. CAL-PEP's outreach services also include support groups held by CAL-PEP outreach workers in a van in the stroll districts. Local prostitutes are invited to come into the van, which is fully equipped with AIDS prevention items, to rest and to talk about how to keep themselves and their clients free of AIDS. In addition, CAL-PEP sponsors monthly workshops in a hotel room in the stroll district for prostitutes and their regular customers, as well as safe-sex workshops at the county jail.[2]

Alexander, who was crucial in getting CAL-PEP launched, anticipated that "CAL-PEP *may* overshadow COYOTE" (personal communication, September 21, 1988). Indeed, a visit to COYOTE's main office in San Francisco reveals that most of the office activities are associated with CAL-PEP. For example, incoming phone calls are directed to CAL-PEP and the majority of the personnel in the office are associated with CAL-PEP. While COYOTE's banner is hanging prominently in the office, occupying the larger portion of one wall, the office activities nonetheless generally reflect the concerns and operations of CAL-PEP. For example, on one occasion in COYOTE's main office, numerous local reporters were present, all of whom either were waiting to interview or were in the process of interviewing office personnel for stories on CAL-PEP.

COYOTE's efforts have clearly taken a backseat to CAL-PEP. According to a report entitled "Prostitutes Lead Fight Against AIDS":

> CAL-PEP has grown from a small grass roots movement consisting of three underpaid, overworked women to a vigorous force for social change responsive to the needs of a chronically misunderstood and stigmatized minority population. . . . CAL-PEP is one of the most vital, energetic forces in the AIDS community. (Hunter 1989, p. 2)

In short, CAL-PEP *has* overshadowed COYOTE.

Alexander's Move to the World Health Organization

Alexander's departure from COYOTE in 1990 marked a new era for COYOTE. Alexander was hired as a consultant for the World Health Organization (WHO) for three months in 1989, and for eleven months in 1990. Since February 1990, Alexander has not been officially affiliated with COYOTE or the NTFP.

Alexander formally left COYOTE to reside in Geneva while working with WHO to develop guidelines for sex work–related AIDS prevention projects that target clients as well as sex workers. As she relayed to me in a letter informing me of her move:

> A small number of AIDS prevention projects have put priority on reducing the amount of prostitution, but most have been focusing on improving the ability of prostitutes/sex workers to work safely. Several members of the ICPR have been working with the World

> Health Organization, and with health organizations in their own countries to develop workable AIDS policies related to sex work, including [a list of prostitutes' rights advocates from around the world]. . . . Prostitutes have been hired as educators, and have developed and run independent AIDS prevention projects on every continent, often as a result of the manual I wrote for CAL-PEP, *Prostitutes Prevent AIDS: A Manual for Health Educators*. Although the manual is very U.S. focused, I have been surprised to find that people in Asia and Africa have found it useful. (February 22, 1990)

Through her work with COYOTE, the NTFP, and CAL-PEP, Alexander has increasingly became recognized as an expert on prostitutes and AIDS. Combined with a growing concern with the role of prostitution in the spread of AIDS, this recognition effectively resulted in Alexander's departure from her position as codirector of COYOTE. Gloria Lockett, who has been the other Co-Director of COYOTE since 1986, is also currently preoccupied with AIDS education in her position as project director for CAL-PEP.

In effect, the current conceptualization of AIDS as a social problem connected to prostitution has served to leave COYOTE without an active leadership, blur the organizational agenda, and drain personnel. As Alexander conceded in a personal interview, "if it weren't for AIDS, the prostitutes' rights movement would be right on target. . . . Because we are focused on AIDS, we don't have time for COYOTE" (September 21, 1988).

RECONSTITUTING THE MOVEMENT

Clearly, the AIDS crisis significantly reshaped the course of COYOTE's crusade. It has resulted in moving the prostitutes' rights movement away from feminist discourse and into public health discourse. Despite this shift in domain, the ideological grounding of COYOTE's AIDS-related claims remains consistent with those disseminated through participation in legal discourse and through participation in feminist discourse. However, the substance of its claims has increasingly been attentive to the way in which the AIDS epidemic has implicated prostitutes by marking them as diseased women who are a danger to themselves and their communities.

The biological characteristics of AIDS, coupled with the general social construction of the disease as more than a medical issue, served to indict prostitutes for the spread of AIDS. Regardless of whether prostitutes have contracted the HIV virus in disproportionate numbers and/or are transmitting it to the general population, the social response to the AIDS epidemic has rendered prostitutes highly visible as a population worthy of public scrutiny and subsequent legal action. Such scrutiny has come primarily from public health officials and legislators, who have invoked historical connections between prostitution and past diseases to shed contemporary suspicion on prostitutes and their role in the spread of the HIV virus.

In light of the urgency of halting the spread of the HIV virus, public health officials and legislators have been charged with responding to the deadly threats of AIDS. They have done so, at least in part, by proposing and implementing public policy measures that rely upon assessments of prostitutes as contaminated women in order to justify the increased social and legal control of prostitutes (e.g., increases in enforcement of prostitution laws, mandatory testing of those arrested on prostitution charges, quarantining of prostitutes). In the process of being charged with and responding to the AIDS epidemic, public health officials and legislators have emerged to increasingly own public discussions of prostitution as a social problem. Accordingly, the social problem of prostitution has recently been more firmly anchored in a concern over public health than a concern about violence against women.

COYOTE has been quick to respond to the emergent view of prostitutes as deadly pools of contagion and the policy proposals deriving from such a view. From the mid-1980s on, the prostitutes' rights movement has been preoccupied with dismantling the conceptualization of prostitutes as contractors, carriers, and transmitters of the HIV virus. In an effort to do so, COYOTE has undertaken numerous campaigns that target public health officials, as well as local and state legislators. These campaigns have challenged public policy responses to AIDS by pressing claims about prostitutes' lower HIV infection rates, as well as prostitutes' historic attentiveness to monitoring their health and the health of their clients. Combined, these claims support the larger effort to construe public officials' response to AIDS as one of political scapegoating; in this case, it is the scapegoating of prostitutes and other marginalized populations. With this view of the problem in hand, COYOTE has become recognizable as a watchdog organization engaging in a defensive crusade to defend prostitutes against frequently proposed and increasingly adopted legislation.

At the same time, as the AIDS epidemic reached alarming proportions, prostitutes' organizations such as COYOTE found themselves in a position to work *with* public health officials by providing assistance in the form of (1) access to prostitutes who may need AIDS education, (2) advice about how to effectively educate prostitutes about AIDS prevention, and (3) valuable information through which to reach the often hidden world of prostitution. As Alexander described:

> We have been contacted by public health departments and AIDS projects around the country requesting information on how to develop AIDS prevention projects. The first thing we say is that the most important element to a successful program is to hire prostitutes to develop and staff the project, and surprisingly, most agree to this. And so, for the first time in history, experience as a prostitute is becoming a requirement for legitimate employment. (1988, p. 172)

The urgency of AIDS has forced the research and health education world to embrace a group of women that they may not have otherwise encountered, and certainly would not have considered peers.

This shift in focus and goals has had a significant impact on the types of activities that COYOTE has come to sponsor and protest. By extension, it has affected the course of the contemporary prostitutes' rights movement. It has lead to the demise of the prostitutes' rights movement per se, and the establishment of prostitutes' rights organizations and their leaders as a critical link between public health agencies and sex workers. Unlike COYOTE's participation in feminist discourse, which was characterized by heated debate and tenuous allegiance, its participation in public health discourse is characterized by acrimonious debate and coaptation.

In an effort to attend to the threats posed by AIDS, the prostitutes' rights movement has at best circumvented and at worst abandoned its original goal. That is, the prostitutes' rights movement has turned away from the pursuit of the repeal of prostitution laws and the celebration of prostitution to join the public health field in efforts to combat the spread of AIDS. In the process, it has become recognizable as an extension of public health's efforts to combat the spread of the HIV virus. Insofar as this is the case, and borrowing from Best once again, the movement's standing as "insider claims-makers" (1990, pp. 13–16) was significantly enhanced as it inherited an opportunity to work within the system in a socially sanctioned way.

NOTES

1. After "The Today Show"s switchboard lit up, host Bryant Gumbel apologized to the viewing audience for presenting such a controversial subject. Two and a half years later, COYOTE representatives appeared on "The Today Show"

for the second time. On this occasion, not only did they discuss the importance of condom use, they also displayed a variety of types of condoms on the air. This time, however, Bryant Gumbel offered no apology to his viewing audience.

2. For a more detailed description of the operations of CAL-PEP, see "Girlfrens: A Study of AIDS Prevention for Street Prostitutes" (1989) by Dorfman, Hennessey, Lev, and Reilly.

6

In Search of Legitimation: A Reprehensible Social Movement Operating in a Yoke of Disreputability

INTRODUCTION

Rather than point to and account for the many ways in which the prostitutes' rights movement has failed, which would be an empirical and theoretical task that has already been undertaken (Weitzer 1991), this chapter focuses on the limited success of the prostitutes' rights movement by accounting for its (quite) unexpected longevity, visibility, and viability. In an effort to do this, I make use of the description of the prostitutes' rights movement's twenty-year crusade that has been detailed in previous chapters. By considering the ways in which COYOTE's claims have been formulated, disseminated, received, and reacted to, my analytic focus is primarily on processes of legitimation and institutionalization. In this way, I respond to one of the key questions raised in the introduction of this book. Namely, how does the movement operate in the shadows of ill repute while trying to diminish those shadows?

Drawing heavily upon a conceptualization of legitimation and institutionalization found in the organizations literature, in this chapter I identify mechanisms through which COYOTE has received legitimation, and has thus gained visibility and support for the prostitutes' rights movement. In order to understand these processes, a section on the nature of legitimation and institutionalization processes is followed by a conceptualization of COYOTE as an example of deviants' organizations. Then, an examination of five processes by which the leaders of COYOTE have sought legitimation for their organization, and by extension their cause, is presented.

LEGITIMATION AND INSTITUTIONALIZATION

A central argument in the organizations literature is that organizational legitimacy is a primary resource for any organization, whether it is a bureaucratic, reform, service, or economic organization (McCarthy and Zald 1973, 1977; Meyer and Rowan 1977; Perrow 1986; Pfeffer 1981, 1982; Pfeffer and Salancik 1978; Scott 1981, 1983; Weber 1947). Organizations must, to varying degrees, attend to obtaining and maintaining legitimation. When they are viewed as illegitimate, attacks from the environment can threaten their survival, efficiency, and effectiveness. With regard to social movement organizations in particular, an understanding of how organizations establish, secure, and lose legitimation is crucial to a general understanding of the evolution of the larger social movement they represent.

Legitimation refers to the degree of cultural support for an organization and the extent to which its existence, goals, and activities are justified to a peer or subordinate system (Maurer 1971; Meyer and Scott 1983). Organizations and their attendant social movements are continuously assessed by their environments for the appropriateness of their goals and activities. Thus, legitimation is best conceived of as an ongoing process, one in which degrees of legitimacy are conferred upon organizations and their social movements by specific constituencies and across particular contexts. Varying constituencies and contexts ensure that the acquisition of organizational legitimacy is ultimately bound up with the social norms and values present in the environment of the organization at any given moment.

Institutionalization

The issue of organizational legitimacy is intimately connected to processes of institutionalization. The concepts of institution, institutionalized, and institutionalization have been defined in diverse ways and with substantial variation among approaches. However, and without agreeing on the specifics, Wuthnow (1987) and others (Perrow 1986; Scott 1987; Selznick 1957; Zucker 1977, 1983, 1987) have concurred that institutionalization, the process of becoming an institution, involves some degree of legitimacy with respect to societal values and procedural norms. As Selznick used the term, to become institutionalized is to become "infused with value beyond the technical tasks at hand" (1957, p. 17) while adapting to the values of the external society.[1] This process can be applied to groups, organizations, practices, and cultural forms alike.

Regardless of where the focus is applied, institutionalization promotes stability and persistence of structure and/or substance across time and space (Berger and Luckmann 1967; Selznik 1957). As Meyer and Rowan explain, "institutionalization involves the processes by which social processes, obligations, or actualities come to take on a rulelike status in social thought and action" (1977, p. 341). Similarly, Zucker notes that "institutionalization operates to produce common understandings about what is appropriate and fundamentally meaningful" (1983, p. 5).

LEGITIMATION OF DEVIANTS' ORGANIZATIONS

Establishing and securing legitimacy and institutional status for social movement organizations and their movements is always somewhat problematic. However, since legitimation is tied to social norms and values, it is especially problematic for organizations that have members and/or constituents whose status in society is socially defined as deviant. Deviants' organizations are necessarily embedded in layers of stigma, which compounds the challenge of acquiring organizational legitimacy.[2] Organizations associated with deviants and deviance exist in an environment that is hostile toward their members, constituents, and/or goals. Deviants' organizations attend to neutralizing culturally granted illegitimacy, while simultaneously attempting to establish and secure legitimation.[3] Although legitimation is ultimately conferred upon organizations by their environments, organizations can nonetheless engage in undertakings that can increase the likelihood of legitimacy being bestowed upon them (Meyer and Rowan 1977; Meyer and Scott 1983; Pfeffer and Salancik 1978).

It is important to investigate the strategies by which deviants' organizations struggle to receive legitimation from the environment for at least three reasons. First, legitimation is closely connected to organizational and social movement survival (Perrow 1986; Pfeffer 1981, 1982; Pfeffer and Salancik 1978). Second, attention to enhancing organizational legitimation has consequences for the goals and functioning of organizations (Meyer and Rowan 1977; Scott 1981, 1983; Weber 1947), especially for social movement organizations (McCarthy and Zald 1973, 1977). Third, the degree to which deviants' organizations receive legitimation from their environments has consequences for the likelihood of the organization becoming institutionalized and gaining support for its goals and/or its cause. In this case, processes of institutionalization are critical insofar as they increase the likelihood that the substance of COYOTE's discourse continues to be reproduced even as the environment changes, and even as the organization lies dormant.

COYOTE as a Deviants' Organization

COYOTE exemplifies deviants' organizations that struggle with legitimation. Prostitution has historically been organized around concepts of devaluation, dishonor, and degradation. It has been viewed as an affront to sexual sanctities, religious mores, family relations, and public health (Bergman 1988; Brandt 1987; Bullough and Bullough 1978; du Plessix Gray 1992; Goode and Troiden 1974; Lerner 1986; Murphy 1983; Tannahill 1980). Consistently, prostitutes have been depicted as sexual slaves, victimized and contaminated women, and deviant actors (Barry 1979; Brandt 1987; D'Emilio and Freedman 1988; Lockett 1988; Schur 1984). In view of these deeply ingrained negative views of prostitution and prostitutes, attaining legitimation for both is a difficult task.

Since prostitution has, for the most part, never been accepted as a legitimate activity, much less an acceptable professional or occupational one, advocating respectability for the "the world's oldest profession" is fraught with difficulty. By putting forth a philosophy that promotes prostitution and celebrates prostitutes, COYOTE is recognizable as representative of individuals who have been socially and culturally stigmatized, degraded, and segregated by institutionalized definitions. As a result, COYOTE's advocacy work has been shrouded in layers of stigma as its philosophy is generally considered repugnant by the larger society. As previous chapters have detailed, their philosophy has, at times, been viewed as misguided, offensive, and/or threatening by key constituencies. Moreover, their constituency has, at times, been considered in need of help at best, morally inferior at worst, and stigmatized regardless.

Given historical and contemporary images of prostitution and the social standing of prostitutes, COYOTE has had to attend to establishing and securing legitimacy in a environment that has, for the most part, in the first instance granted the organization and its movement illegitimacy. In light of this, COYOTE has sought to make its unpopular philosophy more palatable, its members more honorable, and its organization more acceptable. But how has it pursued this?

Five strategies are evident through which COYOTE leaders have, with greater or lesser success, managed their environment in the pursuit of legitimation for their organization and its cause. COYOTE leaders have sought legitimation, and by extension institutionalization, by (1) establishing and anchoring the organization in San Francisco, which is an environment supportive of deviant activities and organizations; (2) placing the plea to decriminalize prostitution in acceptable political discourse; (3) building coalitions with established organizations and social causes; (4) capitalizing on the AIDS epidemic as an environmental crisis; and (5) institutionalizing the claim that COYOTE and its affiliates are, indeed, organizations *of and for* prostitutes.

GAINING ACCEPTANCE IN A CIVIL ENVIRONMENT

San Francisco has been described as a haven for deviants and a natural experiment in the consequences of tolerating deviance (Becker and Horowitz 1971). The culture of San Francisco provides a fertile ground for the proliferation of deviant activities and organizations (Weeks 1985). Becker and Horowitz argue that San Francisco exemplifies a "culture of civility" in which deviance is not only tolerated, but is also relied upon as a civic resource enjoyed by tourists and residents alike.

San Francisco's culture of civility has historically provided local credibility to politically organized marginalized groups, especially those concerned with vice and victimless crimes, such as prostitution. According to St. James (1983), "San Francisco is the only place I could have started COYOTE 'cause I had a lot of grass roots support." As a San Francisco magazine reported on COYOTE's formation: "It finally had to happen and, characteristically, it's gathering in San Francisco: a glimmer of political and feminist liberation is beginning to illuminate the dark corners of the prostitutes' world" (Ritter 1973, p. 4). In an article entitled "The Oldest Profession Organizes at Last" *Ms. Magazine* recognized that "COYOTE's membership is made up of San Francisco's tolerant citizenry, for whom no button is more 'in' these days than COYOTE's" (Braudy and Thom 1973, p. 17).

During its inception, St. James utilized the support of local celebrities to legitimate COYOTE. She recruited influential San Franciscans to form a fifty-person informal advisory board. For example, the original COYOTE letterhead proudly displayed the names of novelist Herb Gold, feminist writer Kate Millet, feminist lawyer Florence Kennedy, Zen philosopher Alan Watts, actor Peter Boyle, entertainer Tom Smothers, feminist Betty Dodson, San Francisco's liberal sheriff Richard Hongisto, onetime San Francisco art commissioner and noted city maverick Jeremy Ets-Hokin, and labor leader David Jenkins. Although these individuals officially served on COYOTE's original advisory board, their place in the organization was primarily symbolic and titular. Nonetheless, they served to legitimate the organization and enabled it to survive during its formative years and endure a "liability of newness" (Bart 1983; Hannan and Freeman 1977).

As Chapter 3 described, COYOTE's early campaigns centered around protesting illegal discrimination against prostitutes, especially police harassment and entrapment. By opposing police harassment of prostitutes, COYOTE representatives capitalized on the San Francisco gay community's political values and successes to legitimate their campaigns. Prior to the formation of COYOTE, the gay community in San Francisco successfully organized to protest police harassment, at least in part by relying upon claims similar to those eventually adopted by COYOTE.

COYOTE's focus on police harassment as a previously accepted grievance offered COYOTE legitimation from key constituencies. COYOTE members associated their organization and its cause with local politics in order to adapt to the institutional environment. More specifically, COYOTE aligned its actions and goals with local political activity that was already deemed legitimate by key constituencies. In so doing, COYOTE was legitimated insofar as its activities were construed as compatible with existing values and concerns in the local community (i.e., San Francisco).

FRAMING ORGANIZATIONAL DISCOURSE

As Chapter 4 documented, COYOTE advocates the decriminalization and promotion of prostitution by disseminating propaganda that locates the social problem of prostitution firmly in the discourse of choice, service work, and civil rights. COYOTE does this through the dissemination of three interrelated claims. First, COYOTE claims that not all prostitution is forced prostitution, that, in fact, often prostitution is voluntarily chosen. Second, COYOTE claims that prostitution is work and should be as respected (i.e., destigmatized) as any other type of work. Finally, COYOTE claims that to deny a woman the option to work as a prostitute under conditions of her own choosing is a violation of her civil rights.

By invoking and promoting a vocabulary of sex as work, prostitutes as sex workers, and prostitutes' civil rights as workers, the prostitutes' rights movement locates prostitution in the discourse of work and civil rights. As St. James declared over ten years ago, "my goal is to get the 1980 political candidates to address this as a women's and a human rights issue" (Lasky 1979, p. 1). Moreover, "we'll give it [COYOTE] a universal perspective and talk about prostitution as a class issue and a human rights issue" (Bryan 1984, p. 8). Related to this purposeful framing, the way in which COYOTE is identified as an organization promotes the connection between its cause and civil rights more generally. Both COYOTE and the media consistently refer to COYOTE as a civil rights organization, a civil rights advocacy organization, a human rights organization, a women's rights organization, and a prostitutes' rights organization.

The plea to decriminalize prostitution is made more supportable and legitimate by providing a corrective response to something our culture purports to abhor, namely, the violation of individuals' civil rights. As the legal scholar Carol Smart has pointed out:

> [R]ights constitute a political language through which certain interests can be advanced. To couch a claim in terms of rights is a major step towards a recognition of a social wrong. . . . To claim that an issue is a matter of rights is to give the claim legitimacy. It is also the case that to pose an issue in terms of rights is to make the claim popular. (1989, p. 143)

In this case, the denial of women's right to work under conditions of their own choosing and the denial of civil rights based on membership in a particular group constitutes the core civil rights violations. Through the dissemination of discourse promoting this claim, COYOTE becomes primarily identifiable as an advocacy organization concerned with securing and protecting individuals' civil rights, and only secondarily identifiable as an organization encouraging prostitution.

In essence, COYOTE's leaders have promoted their organization by generating statements of their goals in discourse that is found to be acceptable to relevant publics. COYOTE responds to the problem of legitimation by linking the organization's actions to beliefs about how the larger movement's goals lead to values that are socially acceptable. That is, the prostitutes' right movement's goals and actions are expressed in terms that are compatible with existing values that are already viewed as legitimate. To the degree that a social movement's stated goals and activities conform to generally accepted norms and beliefs across relevant constituencies, the organization and its cause are legitimated.

ACQUIRING STATUS VIA COALITIONS

As part of COYOTE's national and international crusade, COYOTE declared itself the National Task Force on Prostitution (NTFP) in 1979. The NTFP was formed as an umbrella organization with the intent of eventually developing a formal network of prostitutes' rights advocacy organizations in the United States. The NTFP was also formed in order to promote legitimacy for COYOTE. As the *Boston Phoenix* reported: "Mail sent on COYOTE stationary wasn't getting responses from the likes of the State Department. So COYOTE has become the more official sounding National Task Force on Prostitution" (Diamant 1981, p. 15). COYOTE and the NTFP are, in essence, the same organization. Through the use of dual labels, they legitimate each other as affiliates.

Concurrent with COYOTE's move to be recognized as a national and international organization with many affiliates, leaders of COYOTE focused on alliance building with other community service organizations and social movement organizations. Over the last twenty years, COYOTE and its affiliates have formed symbolic alliances with many nationally recognized organizations and social causes, including the Wages for Housework Campaign, NOW, the gay and lesbian movement, WHO, the ACLU, the Human Rights Commission, and the Institute of Public and Urban Affairs. In addition, COYOTE has forged associations with an array of local public affairs organizations and causes across the nation, ranging from probation and parole associations, citizen's councils for criminal justice, and health departments to press clubs, YWCAs, and community centers.

Consistent with the evolution of the movement presented in Chapters 3, 4, and 5, COYOTE has also secured affiliations with organizations that share concerns about the place of law in individuals' private lives, the status of women, and public health. As a result, the prostitutes' rights movement began to be associated with existing civil rights, labor, women's, and minority groups' causes. As the *Harvard Crimson* reported:

> COYOTE has attracted the attention of many existing groups, for the issue of prostitutes' rights involves larger social movements. Because women are the main targets of exploitation, it has become a women's issue. Because it is often the minority hookers who get caught first and suffers the most from economic and racial discrimination, civil rights groups have become interested in the movement. (Booth 1976, p. 3)

Symbolic associations with other organizations, and involvement in other social causes, serve to legitimate COYOTE with and across a variety of constituencies. Organizations such as COYOTE can have their operations and goals defined as legitimate by associating with other generally accepted—or at least more accepted—organizations, objectives, and/or institutions. Through strategic interaction with social causes and organizations, focal organizations can legitimize their existence, activities, and goals (Astley and Fombrun 1983). Through symbolic joint ventures, the prostitutes' rights movement has stabilized and legitimized its existence.

CAPITALIZING ON AN ENVIRONMENTAL CRISIS

Despite the multitude of threats that the AIDS epidemic poses for prostitutes, it has nonetheless also served to legitimate prostitutes' rights organizations. Although the AIDS epidemic first and foremost threatens to cement the historical connection between prostitutes and disease in the public's mind, it has also served to simultaneously provide COYOTE and other prostitutes' groups with a public forum for pressing their claims, a way to work within the system, and newfound financial resources.

For COYOTE, this has been done primarily through the formation of CAL-PEP, which was described in Chapter 5. CAL-PEP was awarded a thirty-thousand-dollar grant, which was increased to fifty thousand dollars within the first year, for the purpose of educating street prostitutes about safer sex practices and intravenous drug use hygiene. CAL-PEP has also received funding from the Robert Wood Johnson Foundation, the Centers for Disease Control, the Alameda County Health Department, Northern California Grantmakers, the office of Criminal Justice in San Francisco, and the San Francisco District Attorney's Office. Financial sponsorship from such a broad array of public agencies and institutions served to support COYOTE's crusade via support of AIDS-related education projects.

The AIDS epidemic has also brought public officials and prostitutes' rights organizations together in both direct and indirect ways. As described in the previous chapter, those concerned with AIDS have enlisted the help of prostitutes in investigating the role of prostitution in the spread of the disease, and in undertaking educational campaigns to halt the spread of the disease. In the process, select individuals and organizations charged with attending to the spread of the HIV virus have become increasingly dependent upon prostitutes' rights organizations for resources, including such government agencies such as state legislatures, the Centers for Disease Control, and local departments of health. Individuals representing organizations such as these have turned to prostitutes' rights organizations for assistance in the form of (1) access to prostitutes who could benefit from AIDS prevention education, (2) advice about how to effectively educate prostitutes about AIDS prevention, and (3) valuable information through which to reach the often hidden world of prostitution.

At the same time, as the AIDS epidemic began to spread into the heterosexual population it provided a new audience for COYOTE's claims about prostitution. In addition to public health officials, local and state legislators served as an institutionalized forum for the delivery of claims about prostitution. As early as 1988 Alexander observed that "AIDS has moved us further, the legislature is more willing to talk about AIDS" (personal interview, September 21). However, as described in the latter part of Chapter 5, legitimacy bestowed upon COYOTE as a result of varying responses to the AIDS epidemic has, in many ways, come at the expense of its original goals.

INSTITUTIONALIZING AN ORGANIZATIONAL MYTH

Central to whatever legitimation the prostitutes' rights movement has received has been its ability to promote and sustain the public perception that COYOTE is, indeed, a working prostitutes' organization, that is, an organization made up of prostitutes and their representatives. By purporting to make visible the "invisible constituency" (i.e., prostitutes) for the first time in history, COYOTE has received legitimation in the form of media attention and invitations to speak in public. COYOTE claims to be not only representative of prostitutes' voices, but constituent of them as well. Indeed, one of COYOTE's bylaws is that only active prostitutes can vote on organizational issues.

However, as Chapter 3 suggested, the recruitment of prostitutes has been fraught with difficulty. Prostitutes' fear of being identified publicly as well as their fear of reprisal from law enforcement has limited the number of members in the organization who are working prostitutes. Nonetheless, COYOTE has been successful in *claiming* to recruit prostitutes to advocate reform on their own behalf. With the assistance of secondary claims (Best 1990, p. 19), as early as 1973 St. James reported that "enrollments are phenomenal," and that COYOTE had made contact with 25–30 percent of San Francisco's prostitutes, while enlisting about 10 percent of the city's prostitutes (Bryan 1973b). By the end of 1974, COYOTE boasted a membership of over ten thousand (Metzger 1975; Reinholz 1974), and by 1981 COYOTE leaders claimed to have thirty thousand members, 3 percent of whom were active prostitutes (Smyth 1981, n.p.).[4]

Consistent with these reports, both the mainstream and the so-called alternative media have presented the prostitutes' rights movement in a way that implies the presence of prostitutes in the various organizations. The media have referred to COYOTE as a "self-proclaimed prostitutes' union," "a national organization of hookers," "the biggest pros group in the U.S.," "the first prostitutes' guild," "the first prostitutes' union," "a hookers' union," "a hookers' organization," and "a prostitutes' trade union." Labels such as these strongly imply that COYOTE is an organization *of and for* prostitutes. Moreover, headlines such as those presented in Table 6.1 have also assisted in creating and institutionalizing the image of COYOTE as an organization *of and for* prostitutes.

Contrary to COYOTE's public image, only a small percentage of its members have worked as prostitutes, and an even smaller percentage are active prostitutes who are also active in the organization. On occasion, St. James has admitted that COYOTE is *not* an organization constituted by prostitutes:

Table 6.1. Select Newspaper Headlines Suggesting an Organization with Whores

Headline	*Reference*
Hookers of the World Unite	Craib (1973)
Margo St. James, Prostitutes' Union Organizer	Larkey (1973)
Hookers' Union Says It'll Help	Streem (1973)
Hookers Picket 4 Hotels	Bryan (1973a)
COYOTE: Society's Underdogs Begin Biting Back	Ritter (1973)
The Oldest Profession Organizes at Last	Braudy and Thom (1973)
The Oldest Profession Gets a Union	Farguharson (1974)
Organizing the Oldest Profession	Krassner (1974)
Love's Laborers Organize	Fox (1974)
Hookers Arise!	Anderson (1975)
Hookers in City Seek to Unionize "Oldest Profession"	Cockerham (1976)
Hookers Stand Up for Rights	Epstein (1979)
"Pros" Unite: A New Kind of Union to Help Woman-on-the-Street	Paynter (1975)
Prostitutes' Union to End Persecution	Brown (1974)
Why Unhappy Hookers Huddle	Spears (1974)
Solidarity Sweetheart: Can Hookers Be Happy and Militant?	Kellog (1974)
Loose Women Get It Together: The Pros' Unique Convention	Curtain (1974)
Loose Women No Longer Coy, Just Coyotes	Streem (1976)
Prostitutes Seek Legal Relief	Assoc. Press (1976a)
Hookers to Rise in Washington and Buttonhole Congressmen	Assoc. Press (1976b)
Hookers Reveal "Kiss and Tell" to Lure Legalization Campaign	McNulty (1979)

> That has always been the myth, the media's terminology for their idea of COYOTE. I'm not a working prostitute. I haven't worked for many, many years. Besides, a union for prostitutes is not possible now. One could not even dream of starting a union without opening oneself up to a lot of legal problems. (Rutter 1980, p. 15)

Concurring is an analyst concerned with "Confronting the Liberal Lies About Prostitution":

> Alexander, who has never been in prostitution, is the director and chief spokesperson of both NTFP and COYOTE. Neither organi-

> zation has a visible membership or board of directors. . . . I will assume that they are, in fact, one and the same and as such reflect primarily Alexander's philosophy. (Giobbe 1990, p. 68)

Nonetheless, COYOTE spokespeople have not taken serious or consistent action to debunk the notion that it is an organization *of* prostitutes. On the contrary, organizational leaders have been central in creating and promoting the image of COYOTE as an organization *of and for* prostitutes. As a 1988 edition of *COYOTE Howls* declared on the first page, "most members of COYOTE are either prostitutes or exprostitutes, with a few non-prostitute allies" (*COYOTE Howls* 1988, p. 1).

By purporting to have working prostitutes as members, COYOTE has taken advantage of what may be called "novelty capital." "Real" prostitutes speaking out on their own behalf has generated media attention for COYOTE. As St. James explained:

> Being a spokeswoman for an invisible constituency, which must remain invisible, has its disadvantages. The media are always insisting on a "real" prostitute to interview, and often I am told, "you're atypical, you're not a real whore." (quoted in Jaget 1980, p. 199)

The focus on "real" prostitutes has furthered the prostitutes' rights movement's campaigns by attracting media attention and providing alternative images of prostitutes. To the degree that prostitutes are displayed to the public as "normal," the stigma surrounding prostitution can be diminished, and the legitimacy of the organization enhanced. Indeed, perhaps the most effective way for the organization to promote an image of prostitutes that inverts conventional stereotypes is to present real prostitutes as ordinary, well-adjusted individuals trying to make a legitimate living; in so doing, prostitution is normalized.

By assisting in the creation of this institutionalized organizational image, COYOTE leaders have successfully negotiated and constructed the organization's environment. Sustaining the public perception that active prostitutes are central to the structure and functioning of the organization contributes to organizational legitimation. Moreover, it points to the ways in which the structure and activity of prostitutes' rights groups dramatically reflect the "myths" of its institutional environment, instead of the demands of their work activities (Meyer and Rowan 1977). COYOTE has not only conformed to a ceremonial myth, it has helped shape and produce it as well. As a loosely coupled system (March and Olson 1976; Meyer and Rowan 1977; Pfeffer and Salancik 1978; Weick 1976), COYOTE has built and capitalized on a gap between its official structure (i.e., an organization of prostitutes) and its actual work activities.

ASSESSING LEGITIMATION

Assessing the success and failure of a social movement is not an easy task. This stems, at least in part, because of widespread disagreement over the criteria used to undertake such an evaluation. Once a criterion or set of criteria are adopted, the task is still fraught with difficulty insofar as empirical measures of the status, evolution, and outcomes produced by any given social movement are problematic. Regardless, in large part the success or failure of social movement organizations and their attendant social movement nonetheless depends upon the degree to which they receive legitimation from their environment(s). As described earlier in this chapter, this is especially the case with social movement organizations affiliated with culturally defined deviance and deviants.

For the same reasons that it is difficult to measure the success of a social movement, it is also difficult to accurately assess the degree to which an organization or a population of organizations has received legitimation over time and across constituencies. However, the degree to which COYOTE and its affiliates have achieved legitimation can be understood in two ways: organizational survival and political recognition. Organizational survival and political recognition simultaneously reflect organizational legitimation and serve as a source of future legitimation and institutionalization.

COYOTE, as well as its track record and social remnants, still exists in a field where many other attempts to organize prostitutes' rights organizations have failed. Numerous attempts to organize prostitutes have been blocked by violence or social control. For example, in Thailand a few women tried to organize a union called the Thai Night Guard, but they failed because of family pressure, police harassment, and threats from their managers (Pheterson 1989). In Ireland a prostitute who tried to organize prostitutes was burned to death when her house was set afire (Pheterson 1989).

It is notable that COYOTE has managed to survive as a network of advocacy organizations for prostitutes for twenty years, without a solid funding base. As early as 1980, St. James explained:

> Simply continuing to fight over a period of years, one gains a measure of credibility, collects a pile of information, and learns to handle the media to our advantage. . . . [P]ublicity has educated the public [and] gained us some respectability among community groups. (quoted in Jaget 1980, p. 199)

COYOTE has not only survived, it has been successful on a number of local, national, and international fronts. As described in Chapter 3, by as early as 1977 COYOTE's local successes included (1) the end to quarantining of prostitutes; (2) more serious attempts by public defenders to defend women arrested for prostitution; (3) eligibility of arrested prostitutes to take advantage of the pretrial diversion program to be released on their own recognizance; and (4) support from the San Francisco Department of Health for COYOTE to open a free clinic for prostitutes. As described in Chapters 4 and 5, in the late 1970s and throughout the 1980s, COYOTE's main successes have been (1) public awareness campaigns through local, regional, and national conferences and political activity; (2) coalition building; and most notably (3) national and international recognition as a player in the politics of prostitution. Finally, from the mid-1980s until the present, COYOTE has been successful in being embraced as a crucial link between public health agencies and sex workers, and incorporated into a larger effort to effectively respond to the AIDS epidemic.

Accomplishments such as these indicate that COYOTE and its movement have received legitimation from numerous sources and across a variety of contexts, at least much more so than could have been reasonably expected back in 1973. As a Boston newspaper explained over ten years ago: "Margo St. James and COYOTE are not to be dismissed as kooky California phenoms. She is internationally respected by a global network of whores, ex-whores, and people who support the hooker's right to work" (Diamant 1981, p. 16). Perhaps Priscilla Alexander said it best: "We used to be a joke, now we're not" (personal communication, September 21, 1988).

NOTES

1. Like legitimation, institutionalization is not an absolute, as institutions are never permanently secure (Pfeffer and Salancik 1978).

2. *Deviants' organizations* refers to organizations that are constituted by and/or represent members of society who are generally defined as deviant. This does not necessarily imply that the structure or functioning of the organizations is atypical.

3. The terms *legitimacy* and *legitimation* are used interchangeably to refer to external (i.e., environmental) evaluations of the organization rather than to internal ones.

4. As I explained in Chapter 3, it is impossible to accurately assess how many prostitute, ex-prostitute, and nonprostitute members COYOTE and its affiliates have had at different points throughout their twenty-year effort.

7

A Small But Vocal Movement: Theoretical Implications

The previous pages present COYOTE and its affiliates as a small but vocal movement that has managed to persist as an identifiable form of political activity for two decades, despite minimal financial and cultural resources. They have emerged to constitute the prostitutes' rights movement in an effort to protect prostitutes from public designations of deviance, as well as systems of legal and social control. They have undertaken this by declaring their presence openly and without apology in order to engage in public stigma contests that culminate in presenting prostitutes' behavior as legitimate, while derogating public and legal norms surrounding prostitution as illegitimate.

Shielded by a small but vocal movement, prostitutes' rights organizations have emerged from what DeYoung (1984) calls the "lunatic fringe" into public attention. As Chapter 2 reveals, this represents a first in the history of prostitution, the history of sexual politics, and the history of women. Prior to the emergence of the contemporary prostitutes' rights movement, never before had self-proclaimed prostitutes and their advocates visibly challenged commonly held notions about prostitution, offered proposals for reform, and put forth a view of prostitution that affirms prostitutes' behavior as reasonable *and* moral.

COYOTE has rejected the diagnosis of prostitutes' various conditions in an effort to challenge dominant views of prostitution as a social problem. As Chapter 3 describes, COYOTE's grass roots efforts pointed to laws that prohibit prostitution, as well as local law enforcement's selective and discriminatory procedures for enforcing such statutes. This focus culminated in identifying and promoting the law as the primary source of victimization of prostitution. Consistent with the analysis presented in Chapter 4, COYOTE's national and international campaigns marked the establishment of a bona fide prostitutes' rights movement. By joining other feminists in public discussions about violence against women as a social problem, representatives of the prostitutes' rights movement refuted dominant feminist analyses of prostitution. Specifically, the prostitutes' rights movement contested existing images of prostitutes as sexual slaves who are necessarily victimized by commercialized sex and the larger patriarchal context within which it occurs. In essence, the prostitutes' rights movement claims that it is archaic views such as these that are a primary source of oppression to prostitutes in particular and women in general. Finally, as Chapter 5 describes, as the AIDS epidemic reached alarming proportions, the contemporary prostitutes' rights movement targeted public health officials and legislators in an effort to dispute the emergent view that prostitutes represent deadly pools of contagion and vectors of transmission for the HIV. In this final domain of debate, the primary source of victimization of prostitutes ultimately resides with recent public health and legislative efforts to halt the spread of the disease, which in essence render prostitutes political scapegoats.

Clearly, throughout its twenty-year crusade COYOTE has engaged in *diagnostic framing*, which is the "identification of a problem and the attribution of blame or causality" (Snow and Benford 1988, p. 200). It has done so by engaging in public debate primarily with legislators and law enforcement officials, feminists, and public health officials over the source of the problem of prostitution. In the process of addressing the problem of prostitution, the prostitutes' rights movement has focused on the problem with law, the problem with feminism, and the problem with the public response to the AIDS epidemic.

While the identification and acknowledgment of problematic conditions or undesirable conditions is a necessary element in the process of defining or *re*defining social phenomena, it is not a sufficient element. As Klapp has noted, "the symbolic task [of any] movement is to construct new meanings and values" (1972, p. 340). Unlike Gusfield's (1967) repentant deviant, representatives of the prostitutes' rights movement have developed a fairly radical critique of popular views of prostitution by challenging historically developed and contemporary images of prostitution, while at the same time putting forth a new image of the prostitute.

As the previous chapters suggest, COYOTE and its supporters have shaped the symbolic landscape surrounding prostitution by defining the social problem of prostitution as primarily a women's and a civil rights issue. They have done so by invoking and institutionalizing a vocabulary of sex as work, prostitutes as sex workers, and prostitutes' civil rights as workers. This severs the social problem of prostitution from its historical association with crime, illicit sex, and disease. At the same time, it places the social problem of prostitution firmly in the rhetoric of women's work and civil rights. Indeed, one of the most notable features of COYOTE's crusade in general and its claims in particular is how little both are located in and reflect discussions of sex, which has certainly been one the most salient concepts connected to prostitution throughout time and across cultures (Bullough and Bullough 1978).

The prostitutes' rights movement has promoted an image of prostitutes as voluntary service workers whose civil rights are being violated by existing antiprostitution laws, as well as emergent public health–related legislation. Given this, the prostitutes' rights movement is recognizable as an advocate for a select group of women's rights of citizenship, especially their right to work under conditions of their own choosing, and more recently, their right to be free from selectively imposed mandatory testing for the HIV infection and subsequent unduly harsh legal penalties for the spread of the HIV. Seen in these terms, the prostitutes' rights movement has engaged in *prognostic framing*, which is the process of suggesting solutions to public problems (Snow and Benford 1988, p. 201). In this case, the solution includes the decriminalization of prostitution, the protection of prostitutes' civil rights as women and as service workers, and the recognition that prostitution is a credible line of service work.

In framing the social problem of prostitution in this manner, the prostitutes' rights movement *threatens* to take "ownership" (Gusfield 1975) of the problem of prostitution away from traditional experts, especially law enforcement agents, contemporary feminists, and public health officials. It has done so by publicly questioning whose morals are worthy of public affirmation and whose life-styles are deserving of public condemnation and legislative control. In the process, the validity of public and legal designations of prostitutes has been rendered debatable. As du Plessix Gray noted in her recent review of three books on prostitution, "'Sex work,' . . . it is now fashionable to call the profession" (1992, p. 32). When terminologies change, when new terms are invented, or when existing terms are given new meanings, actions are signaled that the career of a social problem is in jeopardy of being reconstructed or deconstructed. After all, the employment of certain categories and meanings over others has direct consequences for the ways in which phenomena are conceived, evaluated, and treated. In this case, what has been construed as a sin in the past and criminal today is currently being fought over as possibly legitimate in the future.

The status of prostitution as a social problem certainly remains open-ended.[1] It remains to be seen, for example, whether or not COYOTE's vocabulary and its associated imagery will be institutionalized (e.g., "sex work" and "voluntary prostitution") and whether or not concepts of the opposing groups will fall into obscurity (e.g., prostitutes as criminals, sexual slaves, and diseased women). The successes and failures of COY-

OTE's crusade and the degree to which its claims have been or will be adopted by the public is important in two respects. First, at least in part, it will determine the degree to which the activities of COYOTE have fundamentally altered prostitutes' political as well as cultural situation. Second, the impact of the prostitutes' rights movement will contribute to determining the future of prostitution as a social problem—so defined.

Regardless of the future of the social problem of prostitution, COYOTE's lengthy public crusade has, at minimum, been successful in giving an impetus to and sustaining a forum for public *re*evaluation of a social problem. Inciting public *re*evaluation of a social problem is no small feat in a highly competitive "social problems market" (Best 1990, p. 15). This is especially difficult when the effort is undertaken by individuals, groups, organizations, and/or social movements with little to no financial, cultural, and symbolic resources. Clearly, the prostitutes' rights movement exemplifies such a phenomenon. Therefore, this book concludes with some theoretical considerations born of this empirical effort.

THEORETICAL CONSIDERATIONS

The focus on social problems as definitional processes can be located in the work of Blumer (1969, 1971) and Spector and Kitsuse (1973, 1977). Since the 1970s, a theoretically integrated and empirically viable tradition of research has developed along the lines prompted by these scholars. The body of work done in this tradition includes, but is certainly not limited to, Aronson's (1982) work on nutrition, Best's work on missing and threatened children (1987, 1990), Gusfield's (1967, 1975, 1981) work on alcohol and drinking and driving, Conrad's (1975) work on hyperactivity, Pfohl's (1977) work on child abuse, a number of works on alcoholism (Chauncey 1980; Schneider 1978), Markle and Troyner's (1979) work on cigarette smoking, Fishman's (1978) work on crime, Richardson, Best, and Broomley's (1991) work on the satanism scare, Rose's (1977) work on rape, and Rafter's (1992) work on the first eugenics campaign in the United States.

Regardless of the specific substantive topic, empirical works such as these share a focus on how certain phenomena in society come to be defined and viewed as problematic by some portion of the citizenry, and ultimately granted the status of "social problem" by the general public. In the main, this tradition has focused on such things as claims-makers, claims-making, rhetoric, mobilization of resources, the media, and the ownership of issues. This focus has, in turn, served as a foundation for the investigation of how larger processes of recognition, identification, and labeling are crucial to the *construction* of social problems.

However, this vein of research has failed to focus on how extant social problems get *reconstructed*, especially by marginalized and stigmatized constituencies implicated in the extant construction of the problem. The reconstruction of a social problem implies that the phenomena remain defined as problematic, but on newly introduced and institutionalized grounds.[2] Crusades associated with deviance and deviants exemplify efforts to *re*construct extant social problems that impute deviance to specific populations in society. In this case, the prostitutes' rights movement exemplifies an effort to reconstruct the social problem of prostitution, which has historically institutionalized imputations of deviance to prostitutes.

The remaining pages of this book constitute an effort to understand *some* of the processes through which social problems get reconstructed by advocates of those implicated in the problem. The theoretical focus is on processes underlying the establishment of arenas of debate, the pursuit of "frame alignment" (Snow and Benford 1988; Snow et al. 1986), and the disavowal of deviance. With a consideration of these processes in mind, I conclude this book with a formulation of a "natural history of *reconstructed* social problems" model.

ESTABLISHING ARENAS OF DEBATE

The prostitutes' rights movement has been anchored in three predictable arenas of public debate. As Chapters 3, 4, and 5 describe, legal authorities and law enforcement agents, feminists, and public health officials have constituted the primary targets of COYOTE's efforts. Accordingly, the prostitutes' rights movement has been primarily located in legal discourse, feminist discourse, and public health discourse. As Chapters 2 and 5 demonstrate, these arenas of public debate have been central in constructing historical and contemporary understandings of prostitution as a problematic type of activity and the prostitute as a problematic type of woman. Representatives from these public domains have, at different points in time, been most active and most visible in conferring the status of social problem onto the phenomenon we call prostitution. Thus, these three public domains have historically owned the social problem of prostitution. By extension, they have also owned the meanings being contested by COYOTE and its supporters.

Clearly, organized challenges to imputations of deviance are located in, or at least run parallel to, those sectors of society that are most responsible for the historical and contemporary construction of the social problem that imputes deviance.[3] When multiple institutions and arenas of discourse are responsible for the construction of a social problem that imputes deviance, the domain that most visibly owns the construction of the social problem at any given time becomes identifiable as a primary target for diagnostic and prognostic framing by those attempting to reconstruct the problem. In this case, the primary target of the prostitutes' rights movement shifted as the location of dominant public discussions of prostitution moved from the legal arena to the feminist arena and ultimately to the public health arena. As Chapters 3, 4, and 5 suggest, the discourse emanating from the prostitutes' rights movement necessarily accompanied the dominant public discourse on prostitution into these relevant arenas of debate. Unlike moral crusades engaged in efforts to *construct* social problems, moral crusades engaged in efforts to *reconstruct* a social problem necessarily frame grievances and proposals for reform within the parameters of extant discourse on the previously constructed social problem. This, in turn, requires immoral crusades to participate in fairly predictable arenas of discourse.

PURSUING "FRAME ALIGNMENT"

COYOTE's activities in general and discourse in particular have, more than anything else, been characterized by underlying processes of "frame alignment" (Snow and Benford 1988; Snow et al. 1986). Snow and Benford explain that:

> We use the verb *framing* to conceptualize this signifying work precisely because that is one of the things social movements do. They frame, or assign meaning to and interpret, relevant events and conditions in ways that are intended to mobilize potential adherents and constituents, to garner bystander support and to demobilize antagonists. In an earlier paper, we argued that the mobilization and activation of participants are contingent upon "the linkage of individual and SMO interpretive orientations, such that some set of individual interests, values, and beliefs and SMO activities, goals and ideology are congruent and complementary" (Snow et al. 1986, p. 464). We referred to this linkage as "frame alignment." (1988, p. 198)

Framing efforts can vary considerably depending upon the social location of those undertaking the larger effort, as well as the target of mobilization and influence. However, frame alignment processes nonetheless remain critical to the successful negotiation of the larger sociopolitical environment that crusades of any type must participate in and ultimately be responsive to.

At both the local and the national level, the prostitutes' rights movement has been presented and received as compatible with (select) existing values and concerns. This is not coincidental. Representatives of COYOTE have ongoingly situated the prostitutes' rights movement firmly within larger publicly legitimated issues and community values. As the previous chapters have demonstrated, the prostitutes' rights movement has symbolically and literally tied the plight of prostitutes to principles and beliefs emanating from the gay and lesbian movement, the larger movement to decriminalize victimless crimes, the movement to enhance the status of women in this country and abroad, and the national and international efforts to halt the spread of the HIV.

These issues and their attendant discourse constitute not only the political backdrop for the prostitutes' rights movement, but a rhetorical and cultural resource for it as well. COYOTE has employed, and ultimately capitalized upon, these larger issues by aligning the prostitutes' rights movement with social causes that have previously captured the attention and following of relevant publics. As Chapter 3 describes, the gay and lesbian community in San Francisco had already gained support for visible claims about the inappropriateness of the law's interference in private, consensual sex between adults. At the same time, the movement to decriminalize victimless crimes had gained momentum as it publicly questioned the value of laws prohibiting consensual activities that provide no self-proclaimed victim or complainant, including prostitution. As Chapter 4 reveals, acrimonious debate and sporadic allegiance with the women's movement over the issue of violence against women allowed the prostitutes' rights movement to capitalize on previously proclaimed commitments to "freedom of choice" and the "right to self-determination" to legitimize claims about prostitutes' rights as service workers. This, in turn, allowed the prostitutes' right movement to define the problem of prostitution in relationship to something our culture purports to abhor, in this case the violation of individuals' civil rights. Finally, Chapter 5 demonstrates that the urgency of the AIDS epidemic forced the research and health education world to acknowledge sex workers and their advocates as a critical element in the larger social problem of AIDS. As a result, prostitutes' rights organizations have been embraced as a necessary link in efforts to combat the spread of the HIV, while COYOTE's representatives have inherited an opportunity to work within the system in a socially sanctioned way. The formation of links such as these has facilitated frame alignment insofar as the prostitutes' rights movement has invoked and employed select elements of the ideology underlying these movements and campaigns to justify the reconstruction of prostitution as a social problem along preferred lines. In so doing, COYOTE has ensured that its numerous challenges to adversarial constituencies remain firmly situated in, and thus ultimately bound by, conformity to a subset of values and discursive themes contained in the larger sociopolitical milieu.

The processes of frame alignment underlying COYOTE's crusade have three general, albeit interrelated, features that distinguish it from crusades responsible for the construction of social problems that are *not* embedded in layers of stigma and social control. First, the frame alignment has been constrained by the parameters of the domains of discourse responsible for the extant construction of prostitution as a social problem. Second, the frame alignment of the movement has consistently invoked previously legitimated beliefs, values, and symbols that appeal to constituencies *within* those domains, but not necessarily *across* those domains. This is precisely why the dominant themes in the discourse of the crusade shift when the targeted domain of antagonists shifts. Third, and finally, frame alignment under these conditions has the consequence of disavowing deviance, which is taken up in the following section.

DISAVOWING DEVIANCE

Under the conditions described above, processes of frame alignment first and foremost serve to disavow deviance. The disavowal of deviance enhances legitimation and therefore contributes to the successful negotiation of the larger sociopolitical environment in which immoral crusades must operate. As described in detail in the previous chapter, the successful negotiation of an otherwise hostile environment ultimately serves to facilitate the survival of the organizations and the institutionalization of their cause.

The prostitutes' rights movement has disavowed its constituency's standing as "different" in at least two ways, both of which are congruous with and an outgrowth of the frame alignment processes described in the previous section. First, the prostitutes' rights movement has focused on and promoted similarities between prostitutes and other groups in society, while rendering differences invisible. For example, the prostitutes' rights movement has promoted prostitution as a legitimate activity, one that resembles other types of acceptable service work. Related to this, it has suggested that prostitutes are working women just like other women who sell parts of themselves, including their mind and their talent, for a living. Underlying COYOTE's entire crusade, from the beginning to the present, has been repudiations of prostitutes as "other" women (i.e., downtrodden women in need of legal protection, sexual slaves victimized by the commercialization of sex, and contaminated women threatening their communities with contagion). In essence, COYOTE's claims blur the distinction between "good girls" and "whores." At the same time, the prostitutes' rights movement has sought to demonstrate the ways in which the problems facing prostitutes are similar to the problems faced by other historically marginalized and politically vulnerable groups, especially other participants in victimless crimes, women in a patriarchal society, and an array of minority groups being scapegoated for the spread of the HIV virus.

The second general way in which the disavowal of deviance has been undertaken by the prostitutes' rights movement is via numerous processes of legitimation. The mechanisms through which COYOTE has been legitimated, and has thus gained visibility and support for the prostitutes' rights movement, have already been described in detail in the previous chapter. They can be summarized as follows: (1) establishing and anchoring the movement in a culture of civility; (2) placing the claims of the movement in acceptable political discourse; (3) building coalitions with established organizations and social causes; (4) capitalizing on the environmental crisis; and (5) promoting and institutionalizing an organizational myth.

Certainly, the social processes of legitimation underlying these empirical realities operate with organizations not associated with social movements, social movements not associated with culturally defined deviance, and social movements that are attempting to construct a social problem rather than reconstruct one. However, a review of these processes reveals that they serve a fundamentally different purpose for "immoral crusades" (Weitzer 1991) attempting to reconstruct a social problem. Namely, they serve to disavow the organization's deviant status and activities, as well as the organization's illegitimacy. By extension, they serve to disavow the deviance associated with the movement's constituency and render the efforts of the immoral crusade amenable to institutionalization, even when the social movement organizations lie dormant and/or are defunct.

THE NATURAL HISTORY OF *RE*CONSTRUCTED SOCIAL PROBLEMS

In the tradition of Fuller and Meyer's (1941), and more recently Spector and Kitsuse's (1977, pp. 130–58), efforts to develop a "natural history of social problems," this book concludes with a preliminary formulation of a "natural history of *re*constructed social problems" model. The model is proposed to apply in situations wherein the reconstruction is prompted and sustained by those (and their advocates) implicated in the social problem imputing their deviance.

The theoretical considerations described above, coupled with a general understanding of other so-called immoral crusades that challenge extant constructions of social problems, suggests the following stages in the *re*construction of a social problem:

Stage 1: The mobilization of representatives of a constituency that is somehow implicated in the extant construction of the social problem.

Stage 2: Participation in public arenas of debate that have housed and institutionalized extant constructions of the social problem being contested. Those public domains and institutions that have, at different points in time, been most active and most visible in the extant construction of the social problem are targeted in campaigns to *deconstruct* existing dominant understandings of the social problem.

Stage 3: The dissemination of claims that serve both diagnostic and prognostic framing purposes. Specifically, the source of the problem is challenged, while proposals for reform that are commensurate with that challenge are put forth within and across those domains identified in Stage 2.

Stage 4: Undertaking of ongoing frame alignment processes. Movement representatives present their campaigns and goals in alignment with values and symbols such that conformity to previously legitimated values and principles is enhanced. In essence, literal and symbolic ties to previously legitimated symbols, values, and beliefs produce a visible coattailing effect.

Stage 5: Engagement in the disavowal of deviance, which simultaneously serves as a resource for and product of ongoing frame alignment processes.

Stage 6: A general movement away from an outsider claims-maker status toward an insider claims-making status.

Obviously, these stages and their underlying processes overlap considerably. Although I have enumerated them sequentially for the purpose of clarity, like most social processes they do not necessarily occur in a linear fashion. Moreover, they are not mutually exclusive of processes identified in other approaches to understanding social problems as social movements or social movements per se.[4] However, these stages point to processes whereby legitimation is enhanced and institutionalization rendered possible under the conditions described throughout this book.

This formulation of a model is very tentative. It is certainly incomplete and the stages are, no doubt, in need of empirical testing and subsequent qualification. However, this model is offered as a proposal, one that can be reworked dependent upon subsequent efforts such as this one. As Spector and Kitsuse acknowledged when introducing their original formulation of "the natural history of social problems":

> It should be clearly stated at the outset that our natural history model is *hypothetical*: we do not assert that the generic social problems processes are the empirically derived collective portrait of a large number of individual histories. We share Blumer's view that, in most areas, the empirical groundwork for such an analysis has not been accomplished. Our discussion is an outline of what we think such histories should attend to. It attempts to prime the pump—to arm social problems researchers with a preliminary guide to amassing first cases. As such research materials appear, empirical generalizations will replace these hypothetical exploratory and speculative ventures. We expect that much of this model—perhaps all of it—will disappear under the scrutiny of empirical materials. If so, they will have been replaced by other generalizations that better describe the range of existing individual histories. (1977, p. 141)

The same disclaimer applies to this natural history of reconstructed social problems model. Although this model is not hypothetical insofar as it derives from a fairly detailed examination of the contemporary prostitutes' rights movement, it is nonetheless being presented here first and foremost to prime the theoretical pump.

NOTES

1. From the point of view of this work, the status of any social problem remains open-ended.
2. The *deconstruction* of a social problem, on the other hand, implies the effective dismantling or disavowal of definitions and/or interpretations that deem some set of conditions or social arrangements a social problem entirely.
3. Social problems impute deviance to select groups of people, while at the same time select groups of people are often understood to constitute a social problem. That is, the way in which many social phenomena (e.g., crime, epidemics, poverty) are construed has consequences for the identification and subsequent labeling of particular groups as deviant (e.g., law violators, ill or sick individuals, poor people) and vice versa. Therefore, mounting a challenge to one entails dismantling the other insofar as the two are connected.
4. Some have questioned whether or not the definitional perspective on social problems is sufficiently different from social movements theory to warrant continued attention. Mauss, for example, has argued that it is not, and that social

problems are always outcomes of social movements. He suggests that "the characteristics of social problems are typically also those of social movements" (Mauss 1975, p. 38). Troyner (1984), on the other hand, notes the similarities *and* differences between the definitional approach, the standard structural approach (Smelser 1963), and the more recent resource mobilization approach to social movements (McCarthy and Zald 1973, 1977; Oberschall 1973).

References

Adam, Barry. 1979. "A Social History of Gay Politics." Pp. 285–300 in *Gay Men*, edited by Martin Levine. New York: Harper and Row.

———. 1989. *The Rise of a Gay and Lesbian Movement*. Boston: Twayne.

Albert, Edward. 1986. "Illness and/or Deviance: The Response of the Press to Acquired Immunodeficiency Syndrome." Pp. 163–78 in *The Social Dimensions of AIDS: Method and Theory*, edited by Douglas A. Feldman and Tom Johnson. New York: Praeger.

———. 1989. "AIDS and the Press: The Creation and Transformation of a Social Problem." Pp. 39–54 in *Images of Issues: Typifying Contemporary Social Problems*, edited by Joel Best. Hawthorne, NY: Aldine de Gruyter.

Alexander, Priscilla. 1979. "Kiss and Tell Campaign: A Question of Ethics." *COYOTE Howls* 3(2):4.

———. 1979. "National Decriminalization a Must as Hypocritical, Sexist Vigilante Groups Spring to Action Across the U.S." *NTFP News* (September/October):1, 3.

———. 1983. "Working on Prostitution." Paper prepared for California NOW. Schlesinger Library at Radcliffe College, Cambridge, MA.

———. 1987a. "Prostitution: A Difficult Issue for Feminists." Pp. 184–214 in *Sex Work: Writings by Women in the Sex Industry*, edited by Frederique Delacoste and Priscilla Alexander. Pittsburg: Cleis Press.

———. 1987b. "Prostitutes Are Being Scapegoated for Heterosexual AIDS." Pp. 248–63 in *Sex Work: Writings by Women in the Sex Industry*, edited by Frederique Delacoste and Priscilla Alexander. Pittsburg: Cleis Press.

———. 1988. "A chronology of sorts." Personal files.

Alexander, Priscilla and Margo St. James. 1981. "Prostitutes Question Porno's Legitimacy." *Womenews* 6(1):n.p.

Altheide, D. L. and J. M. Johnson. 1980. *Bureaucratic Propaganda*. Boston: Allyn and Bacon.

Altman, Dennis. 1971. *Homosexual Oppression and Liberation*. New York: Outerbridge and Dienstfrey.

———. 1982. *The Homosexualization of America*. New York: St. Martin's Press.

———. 1986. *AIDS in the Mind of America*. Garden City, NY: Doubleday.

Anderson, Els. 1984. "What Better Place to Discuss Sin and Sex?" *Alameda Times-Star* (February 10):14.

Anderson, Maurica. 1975. "Hookers Arise." *Human Behavior* (January):40–42.

Aronson, Naomi. 1982. "Nutrition as a Social Problem: A Case Study of Entrepreneurial Strategy." *Social Problems* 29:474–86.

———. 1984. "Science as Claims-Making Activity: Implications for Social Problems Research." Pp. 1–30 in *Studies in the Sociology of Social Problems*, edited by Joseph W. Schneider and John I. Kitsuse. Norwood, NJ: Ablex.

Ashley, Beth. 1974. "Unusual Prostitute with a Set of Unusual Ideas." *Marin County Examiner* (October 25):n.p.

Associated Press. 1976a. "Hookers to Rise in Washington and Buttonhole Congressmen." *San Francisco Examiner* (April 20):8.

———. 1976b. "Prostitutes Seek Legal Relief." *St. Louis Post-Dispatch* (June 22):9A.

Astley, W. Graham and Charles Fombrun. 1983. "Collective Strategy: Social Ecology of Organizational Environments." *Academy of Management Review*, 8:576–87.

Barry, Kathleen. 1979. *Female Sexual Slavery*. New York: Basic Books.

Bart, Pauline. 1983. "Seizing the Means of Reproduction: An Illegal Feminist Abortion Collective—How and Why It Worked." *Qualitative Sociology* 4 (Winter):339–57.

Becker, Howard. 1968. "Social Observation and Social Case Studies." Pp. 232–38 in *International Encyclopedia of the Social Sciences*, Volume 11. New York: Crowell.

Becker, Howard and Irving L. Horowitz. 1971. "The Culture of Civility." Pp. 4–19 in *Culture and Civility in San Francisco*, edited by Howard Becker. New Brunswick, NJ: Transaction Books.

Bell, Laurie, ed. 1987. *Good Girls/Bad Girls: Feminists and Sex Trade Workers Face to Face*. Seattle, WA: Seal Press.

Berger, Peter and Thomas Luckmann. 1967. *The Social Construction of Reality*. Garden City, NY: Doubleday.

Bergman, Beth. 1988. "AIDS, Prostitution, and the Use of Historical Stereotypes to Legislate Sexuality." *The John Marshall Law Review* 211:777–830.

Bessmer, S. 1982. "Anti-Obscenity: A Comparison of the Legal and Feminist Approaches." Pp. 167–83 in *Women, Power and Policy*, edited by E. Boneparth. Elmsford, NY: Pergamon.

Best, Joel. 1987. "Rhetoric in Claims-Making: Constructing the Missing Children Problem." *Social Problems* 34:101–21.

———. 1990. *Threatened Children: Rhetoric and Concern About Child-Victims*. Chicago: University of Chicago Press.

Bittner, Egon. 1965. "The Concept of Organization." *Social Research* 32:239–55.

Blumer, Herbert. 1969. "Society as Symbolic Interaction." Pp. 78–90 in *Symbolic Interactionism*, edited by Herbert Blumer. Englewood Cliffs, NJ: Prentice Hall.

———. 1971. "Social Problems as Collective Behavior." *Social Problems* 18:298–306.

Boggan, E. C., M. G. Haft, C. Lister, and J. P. Ripp. 1975. *The Rights of Gay People*. New York: Discus Books.

Booth, Marilyn L. 1976. "New Tricks in the Labor Zone." *Harvard Crimson* (February 18):3.

Brammer, Rhonda. 1974. "Margo St. James: A Loose Woman Talks About Walking the Streets." *Idaho Argonaut* (September 24):2.

Brandt, Allan. 1987. *No Magic Bullet: A Social History of Venereal Disease in the United States Since 1880*. New York: Oxford University Press.

Braudy, Susan and Mary Thom. 1973. "The Oldest Profession Organizes at Last." *Ms. Magazine* (December):17.

Brent, Jonathon. 1976. "A General Introduction to Privacy." *Massachusetts Law Quarterly*, 61:10–18.

Bromley, D. 1986. *The Case Study Method in Psychology and Related Disciplines*. New York: Wiley.

Brown, Jacquelyn. 1974. "Prostitutes Union to End Persecution." *Daily Californian* (May 1):9.

Brownmiller, Susan. 1975. *Against Our Will: Men, Women, and Rape*. New York: Simon and Schuster.

Bryan, James H. 1966. "Occupational Ideologies and Individual Attitudes of Call Girls." *Social Problems* 13:441–50.

Bryan, John. 1973. "Hookers Picket 4 Hotels." *San Francisco Phoenix* (November 8):1–2.

______. 1973. "Hookers Resist Clean-up: COYOTE Campaign Could Expose Alioto's Motive." *San Francisco Phoenix* (September):1, 2.

______. 1974. "Will Supervisors Screw Whores?" *San Francisco Phoenix* (June 27):1, 2, 8.

______. 1984. "Margo St. James: A Hooker for all Seasons." *Pleasure Guide* (June):7–9.

Bullough, Vern and Bonnie Bullough. 1978. *Prostitution: An Illustrated Social History*. New York: Crown.

Butler, Katy. 1974. "On the Trail of Vice: The Crusade Against Sin on the Streets of San Francisco." *San Francisco Bay Guardian* (April 13–26):6, 7.

Caidin, Martin. 1983. *Face to Face*. Videotape, Schlesinger Library at Radcliffe College, Cambridge, MA.

Caruana, Stephanie. 1974. "Honest Women: Or, Everything You Wanted to Know About Prostitution But Didn't Know Who to Ask." *Playgirl Magazine* (June):81–83.

Castonia, Don. 1979. "U.S. Run for the Pleasure of Men, Founder of Prostitute Organization Says." *Post-Crescent* (November 16):B14.

Caughey, Madeline S. 1974. "The Principle of Harm and Its Application to Laws Criminalizing Prostitution." *Denver Law Journal* 51:235–62.

Chauncey, Robert. 1980. "New Careers for Moral Entrepreneurs: Teenage Drinking." *Journal of Drug Issues* 10:45–70.

Cherrington, Tom. 1980. *No Bull: The Tom Cherrington Show*. Videotape, Schlesinger Library, Radcliffe College, Cambridge, MA.

Civil Disobedience Handbook. 1987. Distributed at the National March on Washington for Lesbian and Gay Rights, (October 8–13), p. 1. COYOTE holdings, Schlesinger Library, Radcliffe College, Cambridge, MA.

Clever, Dick. 1973. "Old Professional Casts a Few Stones in Self-Defense." *Seattle Post-Intelligencer* (August 19):A18.

Cockerham, William. 1976. "Hookers in City Seek to Unionize 'Oldest Profession'." *Hartford Chronicle* (January 9):n.p.

Cohen, Judith, Priscilla Alexander, and Constance Wofsy. 1988. AIDS: Public Policy Issues." *AIDS & Public Policy Journal* 3:16–22.

Coleman, Kate. 1975. "The Prostitute Revolution." *Harper's Weekly* (July 18):5–6.

Collins, Randall. 1971. "A Conflict Theory of Sexual Stratification." *Social Problems* 19:3–19.

———. 1981. "On the Micro-Foundations of Macro Sociology." *American Journal of Sociology* 86:984–1014.

Conover, Pamela Johnston and Virginia Gray. 1983. *Feminism and the New Right: Conflict over the American Family.* New York: Praeger.

Conrad, Peter. 1975. "The Discovery of Hyperkinesis: Notes on the Medicalization of Deviant Behavior." *Social Problems* 23:12–21.

Coward, Rosalind. 1983. *Patriarchial Precedents.* London: Routledge and Kegan Paul.

Coyote Howls. 1974. "Policy." 1(1):1–3.

———. 1979. "Kiss and Tell Campaign." 3(2):1.

———. 1988. "What Is COYOTE?" (March 26).

———. 1989. "Awful New Prostitution Laws." (January):1.

Craib, Ralph. 1973. "Hookers of the World Unite." *San Francisco Chronicle* (May 29):2.

Cristallo, John. 1989. "Are Prostitutes the New Typhoid Marys?" "Geraldo Show." Fox Headquarters, 10201 Pico Boulevard, Los Angeles, CA.

Curtain, Andrew. 1974. "Loose Women Get It Together: The Pros' Unique Convention." *San Francisco Examiner* (June):3.

Daly, Mary. 1978. *Gyn/ecology: The Metaethics of Radical Feminism.* Boston: Beacon Press.

Davis, Mike. 1981. "The New Right's Road to Power." *New Left Review* (July–August):128.

de Beauvoir, Simone. 1953. *The Second Sex.* New York: Alfred A. Knopf.

Deckard, Barbara. 1975. *The Women's Movement: Political, Socioeconomic, and Psychological Issues.* New York: Harper and Row.

Delacoste, Frederique and Priscilla Alexander, eds. 1987. *Sex Work: Writings by Women in the Sex Industry.* San Francisco: Cleis Press.

D'Emilio, John. 1983. *Sexual Politics, Sexual Communities: The Making of a Homosexual Minority in the United States, 1940–1970.* Chicago, IL: University of Chicago Press.

D'Emilio, John and Estelle B. Freedman. 1988. *Intimate Matters: A History of Sexuality in America.* New York: Harper and Row.

DeYoung, Mary. 1984. "Ethics and the 'Lunatic Fringe': The Case of Pedophile Organizations." *Human Organization* 43:72–74.

Diamant, Anita. 1981. "Women's Work: Margo St. James on Prostitution." *Boston Phoenix* (April 21):8, 15–17.

Diamond, Irene. 1980. "Pornography and Repression: A Reconsideration." *Signs* 5:686–701.

Donahue, Phil. 1980. "The Phil Donahue Show." P.O. Box 211, Cincinnati, Ohio 45201. [Videotape, Schlesinger Library at Radcliffe College, Cambridge, MA.

Dorfman, Lori, Susana Hennessey, Jane Lev, and Peg Reilly. 1989. "A Study of AIDS Prevention for Street Prostitutes." Paper presented at the annual meetings of the Pacific Sociological Association, Spokane, Washington.

Dorgan, Michael. 1984. "Oldest Profession Holds Its Own S.F. Convention." *San Jose Mercury News* (July 13):17A.

du Plessix, Gray. 1992. "Splendor and Miseries." *New York Review* (July 16): 31–35.

Dworkin, Andrea. 1981. *Pornography: Men Possessing Women.* London: Women's Press.

Echols, Alice. 1983. "The New Feminism of Yin and Yang." Pp. 430–59 in *Powers of Desire: The Politics of Sexuality*, edited by Ann Snitow, Christine Stansell, and Sharon Thompson. New York: Monthly Review Press.

Ehrenreich, Barbara, Elizabeth Hess, and Gloria Jacobs. 1982. "A Report on the Sex Crisis." *Ms. Magazine* (March):61–64, 87–88.

Eisenstein, Zillah R. 1981. "Antifeminism in the Politics and Election of 1980." *Feminist Studies* 11(2):187–205.

Ellis, Kate. 1984. "I'm Black and Blue from the Rollingstones and I'm Not Sure How I Feel About It: Pornography and the Feminist Imagination." *Socialist Review* (May/August):103–25.

Elshtain, Jean Bethke. 1982. "Feminist Discourse and Its Discontents." *Signs* 7:603–21.

______. 1982. "The Victim Syndrome: A Troubling Turn in Feminism." *Progressive* (June):40–47.

English, Deirdre, Amber Hollibaugh, and Gayle Rubin. 1981. "Talking Sex: A Conversation on Sexuality and Feminism." *Socialist Review* (July–August): 43–62.

Epstein, Carol. 1979. "Hookers Stand Up for Rights." *What She Wants* (August):6–8.

Everett, Karen. 1988. "State Bills Outrage Prostitutes." *San Francisco Sentinel* 16(3):n.p.

Farguharson, Duart. 1974. "The Oldest Profession Gets a Union." *Windsor Star* (May 17):n.p.

Ferguson, Ann, Ilene Philipson, Irene Diamond, Lee Quinby, Carol Vance, and Ann Snitow. 1984. "Forum: The Feminist Sexuality Debates." *Signs* 10:106–12.

Ferree, Myra Marx and Beth B. Hess. 1985. *Controversy and Coalition: The New Feminist Movement.* Boston: Twayne.

Fettner, Ann Giudici and William Check. 1985. *The Truth About AIDS: The Evolution of an Epidemic.* New York: H. Hold.

Firestone, Shulamith. 1970. *The Dialectic of Sex: The Feminist Case for Revolution.* New York: Bantam Books.

Fishman, Mark. 1978. "Crime Waves as Ideology." *Social Problems* 25:531–43.

Foucault, Michel. 1980. *The History of Sexuality.* New York: Vintage Books.

Fox, Charles. 1974. "Love's Laborers Organize." *True Magazine* (December):44–48.

French, Dolores (with Linda Lee). 1988. *Working: My Life as a Prostitute*. New York: Dutton.

Friedan, Betty. 1963. *The Feminine Mystique*. New York: Dell.

Fuller, R. and R. Meyers. 1941. "The Natural History of a Social Problem." *American Sociological Review* 6:24–28.

Gagnon, John N. and William Simon. 1973. *Sexual Conduct: The Sources of Human Sexuality*. Chicago: Aldine.

Giddens, Anthony. 1976. *New Rules of the Sociological Method*. New York: Basic Books.

Giobbe, Evelina. 1990. "Confronting the Liberal Lies About Prostitution." Pp. 67–81 in *The Sexual Liberals and the Attack on Feminism*, edited by Dorchen Leidholdt and Janice G. Raymond. New York: Pergamon.

Goffman, Erving. 1963. *Stigma: Notes on the Management of a Spoiled Identity*. Englewood Cliffs, NJ: Prentice Hall.

Goode, Erich and Richard Troiden, eds. 1974. *Sexual Deviance & Sexual Deviants: The Social Side of Sex, Pornography, Prostitution, Male Homosexuality, Lesbianism, Rape, and Kinky Sex*. New York: William Morrow.

Gorner, Peter. 1977. "Prostitutes and Housewives Unite, Forming a Surprising Sisterhood." *Chicago Tribune* (April 18):2.

Griffin, Susan. 1982. *Pornography and Silence: Culture's Revenge Against Nature*. New York: Harper and Row.

Gusfield, Joseph R. 1963. *Symbolic Crusade*. Urbana, IL: University of Illinois Press.

———. 1967. "Moral Passage: The Symbolic Process in Public Designations of Deviance." *Social Problems* 15:175–88.

———. 1968. "On Legislating Morals: The Symbolic Process of Designating Deviance." *California Law Review* 58:54–73.

———. 1975. "Categories of Ownership and Responsibility in Social Issues: Alcohol Abuse and Automobile Use." *Journal of Drug Issues* 5:285–303.

———. 1981. *The Culture of Public Problems: Drinking, Driving, and the Symbolic Order*. Chicago: University of Chicago Press.

———. 1984. "On the Side: Practical Action and Social Constructivism in Social Problems Theory." Pp. 31–51 in *Studies in the Sociology of Social Problems*, edited by Joseph W. Schneider and John I. Kitsuse. Norwood, NJ: Ablex.

Hannan, Michael T. and John H. Freeman. 1977. "The Population Ecology of Organizations." *American Journal of Sociology* 82:929–64.

Harlot, Scarlot. 1987. "The Scarlot Letter." *Bay Area Women's News* (March/April):n.p.

Henkin, William. 1988. "What's a Nice Girl Like You Doing in a Book Like This?" *Spectator* 21 (October 4):3.

———. 1989. "Whores Are People Too." *Spectator* 22 (August 5):4–5, 18.

Hobson, Barbara. 1987. *Uneasy Virtue: The Politics of Prostitution and the American Reform Tradition*. New York: Basic Books.

Hughes, Graham. 1975. *The Conscience of the Courts*. Garden City, NY: Anchor Press/Doubleday.

Hunter, Boyd. 1989. "Prostitutes Lead Fight Against AIDS." *Spectator* (June):2.

Hyde, Janet Shibley. 1982. *Understanding Human Sexuality*. New York: McGraw-Hill.

Jacob, E. 1987. "Qualitative Research Traditions: A Review." *Review of Educational Research* 57:1–50.

Jaget, Claude, ed. 1980. *Prostitutes: Our Life*. Bristol: Falling Wall Press.

James, Jennifer, Jean Withers, Marilyn Haft, and Sara Theiss. 1977. *Politics of Prostitution*. Seattle, WA: Social Research Associates.

Jones, Brian, Bernard Gallagher, and Joseph A. McFalls. 1988. *Social Problems: Issues, Opinions, and Solutions*. New York: McGraw-Hill.

Katz, Jonathan. 1976. *Gay American History*. New York: Crowell.

Keegan, Anne. 1974. "World's Oldest Profession Has the Night Off." *Chicago Tribune* (July 10):1, 19.

Kellog, Mary Alice. 1974. "Solidarity Sweetheart: Can Hookers Be Happy and Militant?" *Chicago Sun Times* (October 6):22–24.

Kennedy, M. 1979. "Generalizing from Single Case Studies." *Evaluation Quarterly* 3:661–79.

Kirzner, Ellie. 1985. "Margo St. James Selling Sex Work." *Now Magazine/Toronto Weekly* n.p.

Kitsuse, John. 1980. "Coming Out All Over: Deviants and the Politics of Social Problems." *Social Problems* 28:1–13.

Klapp, Orrin. 1972. *Currents of Unrest: An Introduction to Collective Behavior*. New York: Holt, Rinehart and Winston.

Klatch, Rebecca. 1987. *Women of the New Right*. Philadelphia: Temple University Press.

Klemesrud, Judy. 1985. "A Personal Crusade Against Prostitution." *New York Times* (June 24):C16.

Krassner, Paul. 1974. "Organizing the Oldest Profession." *Rollingstone Magazine* (August 15):n.p.

Larkey, Michael. 1973. "Margo St. James, Prostitutes' Union Organizer." *California Girl* (June):19–20.

Lasky, Helaine. 1979. "Former Prostitute Speaks Up for the Working Woman." *Alameda Times Star* (January 25):1.

Laws, Judith. 1979. *The Second X: Sex Role and Social Role*. New York: Elsevier.

Laws, Judith Long and Pepper Schwartz. 1977. *Sexual Scripts: The Social Constructions of Female Sexuality*. Hinsdale, IL: Dryden Press.

Lederer, Laura, ed. 1980. *Take Back the Night: Women on Pornography*. New York: William Morrow.

Leidholdt, Dorchen and Janice G. Raymond, eds. 1990. *The Sexual Liberals and the Attack on Feminism*. New York: Teachers College Press.

Leigh, Carol. 1987. "AIDS: No Reason for a Witchhunt." *Oakland Tribune* (August 17):1.

———. 1988. "Further Violations of Our Rights." *October: Special Edition on AIDS* 177–81.

Leonard, Arthur S. 1992. "Gay/Lesbian Rights: Report from the Legal Front." Pp. 313 in *Race, Class and Gender in the United States: An Integrated Study*, edited by Paula S. Rothenberg. New York: St. Martin's Press.

Lerner, Gerda. 1986. *The Creation of Patriarchy*. New York: Oxford University Press.

Lockett, Gloria. 1988. "COYOTE Howls over New Law." *Spectator Magazine* (September 30–October 6):2.

———. 1989. "Are Prostitutes the New Typhoid Marys?" "Geraldo Show." Fox Headquarters, 10201 Pico Boulevard, Los Angeles, CA.

Luxenberg, Joan and Thomas Guild. 1990. "Coercion, Criminal Sanctions and AIDS." Paper presented at the annual meetings of the Society for the Study of Social Problems, Washington, D.C.

MacKinnon, Catherine. 1982. "Feminism, Marxism, Method, and the State: An Agenda for Theory." *Signs* 7:515–44.

———. 1983. "Marxism, Feminism, Method and the State: Toward Feminist Jurisprudence." *Signs* 8:635–58.

Mansbridge, Jane. 1986. *Why We Lost the ERA*. Chicago: University of Chicago Press.

March, James G. and Johan P. Olson. 1976. *Ambiguity and Choice in Organizations*. Bergen, Norway: Universitetsforlaget.

Markle, Gerald E. and Ronald Troyner. 1979. "Smoke Gets in Your Eyes: Cigarette Smoking as Deviant Behavior." *Social Problems* 26:611–25.

Marotta, Toby. 1981. *The Politics of Homosexuality*. Boston: Houghton Mifflin.

Martin, Patricia Yancey. 1990. "Rethinking Feminist Organizations. *Gender & Society* 4:182–206.

Maurer, J. G. 1971. *Readings in Organizations Theory: Open System Approaches*. New York: Random House.

Mauss, A. L. 1975. *Social Problems as Social Movements*. Philadelphia: Lippincott.

McCarthy, J. D. and M. N. Zald. 1973. *The Trend of Social Movements in America: Professionalization and Resource Mobilization*. Morristown, NJ: General Learning Press.

———. 1977. "Resource Mobilization and Social Movements: A Partial Theory." *American Journal of Sociology* 82:1212–41.

McCormack, T. 1978. "Machismo in Media Research." *Social Problems* 25:544–55.

McNulty, Timothy. 1979. "Hookers Reveal 'Kiss and Tell' to Lure Legalization." *Tempo Topics* (n.d.):n.p.

Metzger, Peter H. 1975. "COYOTE Head Promotes the Image of a Healthy Hooker." *Rocky Mountain News* (August 3):8.

Meyer, John and Brian Rowan. 1977. "Institutional Organizations: Formal Structure as Myth and Ceremony." *American Journal of Sociology* 83:340–63.

Meyer, John and W. Richard Scott. 1983. *Organizational Environments: Ritual and Rationality*. Beverly Hills: Sage.

Millet, Kate. 1970. *Sexual Politics*. Garden City, NY: Doubleday.

———. 1971. "Prostitution: A Quartet for Female Voices." Pp. 60–125 in *Women in Sexist Society: Studies in Power and Powerlessness*, edited by Vivian Gornick and Barbara Morgan. New York: Basic Books.

———. 1974. "J, The Life." Pp. 135–48 in *Sexual Deviance and Sexual Deviants: The Social Side of Sex, Pornography, Prostitution, Male Homosexuality, Lesbianism, Rape and Kinky Sex*, edited by Erich Goode and Richard Troiden. New York: William Morrow.

Milner, Richard and Diana Hawkins. 1976. "Prosty Power on the Potomac." Schlesinger Library at Radcliffe College, Cambridge, MA.

Mitchell, Cynthia. 1984. "Inside the Hookers' Convention." *Point Reyes Light* (July 19):10.

Morgan, Robin. 1978. *Going Too Far: The Personal Chronicle of a Feminist.* New York: Vintage Books.

______. 1982. *The Anatomy of Freedom.* Garden City, NY: Doubleday.

Morris, Norval. 1973. "The Law Is a Busy Body." *New York Times Magazine* (April 18):58–64.

Morris, Norval and Gordon Hawkins. 1970. *The Honest Politician's Guide to Crime Control.* Chicago: University of Chicago Press.

Mueller, G. 1980. *Sexual Conduct and the Law.* Dobbs Ferry, NY: Oceana.

Murphy, Emmett. 1983. *Great Bordellos of the World: An Illustrated History.* London: Quartet Books.

Mydans, Seth. 1976. "Attitudes on Prostitution Changing." *New Times* (February 15):n.p.

Nielson, Gary. 1979. "Screwing the System: Local Power Structure Should Be Held Accountable for Their Role in Prostitution, Says Ex-Hooker Activist." *Valley Advocate* 11(13):105, 125.

Oberschall, Anthony. 1973. *Social Conflicts and Social Movements.* Englewood Cliffs, NJ: Prentice Hall.

Otis, Leah Lydia. 1985. *Prostitution in Medieval Society: The History of an Urban Institution in Languedoc.* Chicago: University of Chicago Press.

Overall, Christine. 1992. "What's Wrong with Prostitution? Evaluating Sex Work." *Signs* 17:705–25.

Owens, R. 1982. "Methodological Rigor in Naturalistic Inquiry: Some Issues and Answers." *Educational Administrative Quarterly* 18:2–21.

Packer, Herbert. 1968. *The Limits of Criminal Sanctions.* Stanford, CA: Stanford University Press.

Palmer, Barbara. 1976. "Hookers Cashing in on the 'Liz Ray Thing.'" *Washington Star* (n.d.):n.p.

Pankhurst, J. G. and S. K. Homeknecht. 1983. "The Family, Politics and Religion in the 1980s: In Fear of the New Individualism." *Journal of Family Issues* 4:5–34.

Patton, Cindy. 1990. *Inventing AIDS.* New York: Routledge.

Paynter, Susan. 1975. "'Pros' Unite: A New Kind of Union to Help Woman-on-the-Street." COYOTE Holdings, Schlesinger Library at Radcliffe College, Cambridge, MA.

Perrow, Charles. 1986. *Complex Organizations: A Critical Essay.* New York: Random House.

Pfeffer, Jeffrey. 1981. *Power in Organizations.* Boston: Pittman.

______. 1982. *Organizations and Organizational Theory.* Boston: Pittman.

Pfeffer, Jeffrey and Gerald R. Salancik. 1978. *The External Control of Organizations: A Resource Dependence Perspective.* New York: Harper and Row.

Pfohl, Stephen. J. 1977. "The Discovery of Child Abuse." *Social Problems* 24:310–23.

Pheterson, Gail. 1986. *The Whore Stigma: Female Dishonor and Male Unworthiness.* The Netherlands: Dutch Ministry of Social Affairs and Employment.

______. 1989. *A Vindication of the Rights of Whores*. Seattle, WA: Seal Press.

Rafter, Nicole. 1992. "Claims-Making and Socio-Cultural Context in the First U.S. Eugenics Campaign." *Social Problems* 39:17–34.

Reinholz, Mary. 1974. "The Liberated Woman: Loose Women Unite." *New York Times* (February 3):n.p.

Reiper, Donna. 1982. "Legal Prostitution Said Key to Stopping Rape." *Western Front* (May 7):3.

Richardson, James T., Joel Best, and David G. Bromley. 1991. *The Satanism Scare*. Hawthorne, NY: Aldine de Gruyter.

Ritter, Jess. 1973. "COYOTE: Society's Underdogs Begin Biting Back." *Pacific Sun* (December 20–26):4–5.

Rivera, Geraldo. 1989. "Are Prostitutes the New Typhoid Marys?" "Geraldo Show." Fox Headquarters, 10201 Pico Boulevard, Los Angeles, CA.

Rose, V. M. 1977. "Rape as a Social Problem: A Byproduct of the Feminist Movement." *Social Problems* 25:75–89.

Rosenberg, Charles E. 1962. *The Cholera Years*. Chicago: University of Chicago Press.

Rosenbleet, C. and B. J. Pariente. 1973. "The Prostitution of the Criminal Law." *American Criminal Law Review* 11:373–427.

Rubin, Gayle. 1975. "The Traffic in Women: Notes on the 'Political Economy' of Sex. Pp. 157–210 in *Toward an Anthropology of Women*, edited by Rayna Reiter. New York: Monthly Review Press.

______. 1984. "Thinking Sex: Notes for a Radical Theory of the Politics of Sexuality." Pp. 267–319 in *Pleasure and Danger: Exploring Female Sexuality*, edited by Carol S. Vance. London: Routledge and Kegan Paul.

Rubin, Gayle and Pat Califia. 1981. "Sadomasochism: Fears, Facts, Fantasies." *Gay Community News* 9:7.

Rubin, Sylvia. 1986. "COYOTE's New Leadership." *San Francisco Chronicle* (February 25):n.p.

Rutter, Jared. 1980. "COYOTE'S Margo St. James." COYOTE Holdings, Schlesinger Library at Radcliffe College, Cambridge, MA.

Sacramento Bee. 1990. "No Murder-Try Case for Addicted Hooker." (July 18):B7.

San Francisco Magazine. 1973. "COYOTE: A Loose Woman's Organization." (June):23.

Schlesinger Library Holdings. No date. COYOTE Holdings at the Schlesinger Library at Radcliffe College, Cambridge, MA.

Schneider, Joseph. 1978. "Deviant Drinking as Disease: Alcoholism as Social Accomplishment." *Social Problems* 25:361–72.

______. 1984. "Morality, Social Problems, and Everyday Life." Pp. 180–206 in *Studies in the Sociology of Social Problems*, edited by Joseph W. Schneider and John I. Kitsuse. Norwood, NJ: Ablex.

______. 1985. "Social Problems Theory: The Constructionist View." *Annual Review of Sociology* 11:209–29.

Schneider, Joseph and John I. Kitsuse. 1984. *Studies in the Sociology of Social Problems*. Norwood, NJ: Ablex.

Schur, Edwin. 1965. *Crimes without Victims: Deviant Behavior and Public Policy*. Englewood Cliffs, NJ: Prentice Hall.

______. 1984. *Labeling Women Deviant: Gender, Stigma, and Social Control.* New York: Random House.

Scott, Richard. 1981. *Organizations: Rational, Natural, and Open Systems.* Englewood Cliffs, NJ: Prentice Hall.

______. 1983. "Reform Movements and Organizations: The Case of Aging." Pp. 115–28 in *Organizational Environments: Ritual and Rationality,* edited by John W. Meyer and Richard Scott. Beverly Hills: Sage.

______. 1987. "The Adolescence of Institutional Theory." *Administrative Science Quarterly* 32:493–511.

Seidman, Steven. 1992. *Embattled Eros: Sexual Politics and Ethic in Contemporary America.* New York: Routledge.

Selznik, Philip. 1957. *Leadership in Administration.* New York: Harper and Row.

Sheehy, Gail. 1974. "The Economics of Prostitution: Who Profits? Who Pays?" Pp. 110–23 in *Sexual Deviance and Sexual Deviants: The Social Side of Sex, Pornography, Prostitution, Male Homosexuality, Lesbianism, Rape and Kinky Sex,* edited by Erich Goode and Richard Troiden. New York: William Morrow.

Silver, Carol Ruth. 1974. "COYOTE Quotes." *COYOTE Howls* 1(1):1–3.

Smart, Carol. 1989. *Feminism and the Power of Law.* New York: Routledge.

Smelser, N. 1963. *Theory of Collective Behavior.* New York: Free Press.

Smyth, Elaine. 1981. "For Prostitutes, Safe Streets?" *San Diego Union* (February 25):n.p.

Snider, Burr. 1976. "The Gospel of Sex According to Margo St. James." *OUI* 5(2):73–74, 159–62.

Snitow, Ann, Christine Stansell, and Sharon Thompson, eds. 1983. *Powers of Desire: The Politics of Sexuality.* New York: Monthly Review Press.

Snow, David A. and Robert D. Benford. 1988. "Ideology, Frame Resonance, and Participant Mobilization." *International Social Movements Research* 1:197–217.

Snow, David A., E. Burke Rochford, Jr., Steven K. Worden, and Robert Benford. 1986. "Frame Alignment Processes, Micromobilization, and Movement Participation." *American Sociological Review* 51:464–81.

Sontag, Susan. 1977. *Illness as Metaphor.* New York: Farrar, Straus and Giroux.

Spears, Lawrence M. 1974. "Why Unhappy Hookers Huddle." *National Observer* (July 6).

Spector, Malcolm. 1977. "Legitimizing Homosexuality." *Society* 14:20–24.

______. 1981. "Beyond Crime: Seven Methods for Controlling Troublesome Rascals." Pp. 127–58 in *Law and Deviance,* edited by H. L. Ross. Beverly Hills: Sage.

Spector, Malcolm and John I. Kitsuse. 1973. "Social Problems: A Reformulation." *Social Problems* 21:145–90.

______. 1977. *Constructing Social Problems.* Menlo Park, CA: Cummings.

St. James, Margo. 1973. "Prostitutes as Political Prisoners." *Realist* (n.d.):9.

______. 1980. "COYOTE Howls: Margo Visits Netherlands, Finds 'Sexual Slavery' Author Bigoted." *San Francisco's Appeal to Reason* (n.d.):7.

St. James, Margo and Priscilla Alexander. 1977. "Prostitution: The Feminist Dilemma." *City Magazine* (October/November):n.p.

______. 1985. Testimony on prostitution, given to the New York State Bar Association, October 30.

Stake, R. 1978. "The Case Study Method in Social Inquiry." *Educational Researcher* 7:5–8.

Stivision, David. 1982. "Homosexuals and the Constitution." Pp. 303–21 in *Homosexuality*, edited by William Paul, James D. Weinrich, John C. Gonsiorek, and Mary Hotvedt. Beverly Hills: Sage.

Streem, Kathie. 1973. "Hookers' Union Says It'll Help." *Berkeley Barb* (July 6–12):n.p.

———. 1976. "Loose Women No Longer Coy, Just Coyotes." COYOTE Holdings, Schlesinger Library at Radcliffe College, Cambridge, MA.

Strong, Ellen. 1970. "The Hooker." Pp. 289–96 in *Sisterhood is Powerful: An Anthology of Writings from the Women's Liberation Movement*, edited by Robin Morgan. New York: Vintage Books.

Tannahill, Ray. 1980. *The History of Sex*. New York: Stein and Day.

Terzian, Sandra. 1974. "The Real Victim." *COYOTE Howls* (October/November):3.

Thomas, Stephanie. 1978. "COYOTE Energy = Social Change." *COYOTE Howls* (Winter):8.

Tremblay, Johanne. 1988. "Prostitution Is Not a Profession." *WHISPER* (Spring):1, 4.

Troyer, Ronald J. 1984. "Better Read Than Dead: Notes on Using Archival Material in Social Problems and Deviance Research." Pp. 1–30 in *Studies in the Sociology of Social Problems*, edited by Joseph W. Schneider and John I. Kitsuse. Norwood, NJ: Ablex.

Vance, Carol S. 1982. "Concept Paper: Towards a Politics of Sexuality." Pp. 38–40 in *Diary of a Conference on Sexuality*, edited by Hannah Aldeyer, Beth Jaker, and Marybeth Nelson. New York: Faculty Press.

———. 1984. *Pleasure and Danger: Exploring Female Sexuality*. London: Routledge and Kegan Paul.

Viguerie, Richard. 1980. *The New Right: We're Ready to Lead*. Falls Church, VA: Author.

Volinn, Ilse J. 1983. "Health Professionals as Stigmatizers and Destigmatizers of Diseases: Alcoholism and Leprosy As Examples." *Social Science and Medicine* 17:385–93.

Volz, Joseph. 1976. "Hookers' Lobbyist Aims Her Legal Hustle at D.C." *Daily News* (June 22):14.

von Hoffman, Nicholas. 1974. "COYOTE, ASP, PONY and Other Such in the Nut Capital." *Washington Post* (May 27):n.p.

Wages for Housework. 1977. *Newsletter* (Spring):8.

Walkowitz, Judith R. 1980. *Prostitution and Victorian Society: Women, Class and the State*. Cambridge: Cambridge University Press.

———. 1983. "Male Vice and Female Virtue: Feminism and Politics of Prostitution in Nineteenth Century Britain." Pp. 419–38 in *Powers of Desire: The Politics of Sexuality*, edited by Ann Snitow, Christine Stansell, and Sharon Thompson. New York: Monthly Review Press.

Weber, Max. 1947. *The Theory of Social and Economic Organizations*, translated by A. H. Henderson and Talcott Parsons. Glencoe, IL: Free Press.

Weeks, Jeffrey. 1985. *Sexuality and Its Discontents: Meanings, Myths & Modern Sexualities*. Boston: Routledge and Kegan Paul.

Weick, Karl E. 1976. "Educational Organizations as Loosely Coupled Systems." *Administrative Science Quarterly* 21:1–19.

Weitzer, Ronald. 1991. "Prostitutes' Rights in the United States: Failure of a Movement." *Sociological Quarterly* 32:23–41.

Willis, Ellen. 1981. "Lust Horizons: Is the Women's Movement Pro-Sex?" *Village Voice* (June):n.p.

______. 1982 "Who Is a Feminist? A Letter to Robin Morgan." *Village Voice* (December):17.

______. 1983. "Feminism, Moralism, and Pornography." Pp. 460–67 in *Powers of Desire: The Politics of Sexuality*, edited by Ann Snitow, Christine Stansell, and Sharon Thompson. New York: Monthly Review Press.

Wilson, W. Cody. 1973. Pornography: The Emergence of a Social Issue and the Beginning of Psychological Study." *Journal of Social Issues* 29:7–17.

Winklebleck, Layne. 1988. "COYOTE Howls over New Law!" *Spectator* 21(1):2.

World Wide Whore's News. 1985. "Prostitutes and AIDS." (June 19):1.

Wuthnow, Robert. 1987. *Meaning and Moral Order: Explorations in Cultural Analysis*. Berkeley: University of California Press.

Yin, Robert. 1981. "The Case Study as a Serious Research Strategy." *Knowledge: Creation, Diffusion, and Utilization* 3:97–114.

______. 1981. "The Case Study Crisis: Some Answers." *Administrative Science Quarterly* 26:58–65.

______. 1984. *Case Study Research: Design and Methods*. Newbury Park, CA: Sage.

Young, Wayland. 1964. *Eros Denied*. New York: Grove Press.

Zeeck, David. 1976. "Prostitution Law Racist, Sexist." *Kansas City Star-Times* (April 20):n.p.

Zimmerman, Don and Melvin Pollner. 1970. "The Everyday World as Phenomena." Pp. 80–103 in *Understanding Everyday Life*, edited by Jack Douglas. London: Routledge and Kegan Paul.

Zucker, Lynne G. 1977. "The Role of Institutionalization in Cultural Persistence." *American Sociological Review* 42:726–43.

______. 1983. "Organizations and Institutions." *Research in the Sociology of Organizations* 2:1–47.

______. 1987 "Institutional Theories of Organizations." *Annual Review of Sociology* 13:443–64.

Index